THE GREATEST SECRET
IN
LALITA SAHASRANAMA

DEEPIKA ARORA

THE GREATEST SECRET IN LALITA SAHASRANAMA

**Lalita is the joyful dynamic and sparkling expression
of the Self
A free consciousness well founded in the Self**

**śrīmahātripurasundarīṃ śrīvidyāṃ śrīlalitāmbikāṃ
kāmeśīṃ parameśvarīṃ śrīcakreśvarīṃ namāmi**

**I bow to the Supreme Goddess, the beauty of the three
worlds, the source of all knowledge, the auspicious Lalita, the
one who fulfills desires, the supreme ruler, the queen of the
Sri Chakra**

This book is dedicated to you

ACKNOWLEDGEMENTS

The Divine Source has been the cornerstone of this book's creation. Without divine influence, the inspiration and creativity necessary to bring this work to life would have been unattainable. I am eternally grateful for divine guidance and support throughout this journey.

I am also deeply indebted to my family and well-wishers. Their unwavering belief in me and their constant encouragement have been invaluable. Their love and support have provided a steadfast foundation, fueling my determination to complete this book. Their presence has been a true blessing, and I am forever grateful for their role in making this dream a reality.

CONTENTS

The Body, a gadget, its purpose defined,
The Mind, its software, intricately entwined,
Food, Meditation, Yoga and Sleep, the charge it receives,
While you, the consciousness, Where true spirit weaves,
A radiant spark, beyond all the worldly reign.

ABOUT THE BOOK

> A cosmic tapestry, woven with grace,
> A celestial guide in every space.
> A haven of peace, a guiding light
> A radiant source, shining bright.

Life's journey is often marked by challenges. Despite possessing degrees and skills, I found myself grappling with relationship issues and financial constraints. These difficulties, however, became catalysts for personal growth. For over two decades, I lived unaware of my true potential, but the path to self-discovery was eventually illuminated.

Drawn to the spiritual practices of South India, I was captivated by the Lalita Sahasranama, a sacred hymn dedicated to the Divine Feminine. Through diligent study and meditation, I embarked on a transformative journey. Sleepless nights and vivid dreams guided me towards a profound realization: "We are miniatures of the universe."

The success of my debut book, **'THE SECRET IN LALITA SAHASRANAMA'** fueled my desire to explore more of the profound wisdom contained within the Lalita Sahasranama. I have crafted this work to unveil the hidden wisdom within the ancient text. By focusing on the initial 23 verses, I aim to shed light on our true selves, aligning with the fundamental principle of Vedanta philosophy - 'Aham Brahmasmi' (I am Brahman).

To enhance your spiritual practice, the book includes the complete Lalita Sahasranama hymn for chanting. Additionally, a section exploring the transformative potential of this sacred text is provided to encourage deeper reflection and meditation.

In this book, I invite you to join me on this transformative journey. Lets together, explore the depths of Lalita Sahasranama, a sacred text that holds the key to unlocking our inner potential. By understanding the profound wisdom contained within its verses, we can awaken to our true nature, break free from the limitations of the mind, and experience the boundless joy of liberation.

Best of luck on your journey. May the universe grant you both material and spiritual prosperity.

Part I
Introduction to Sri Vidya and Lalita Sahasranama

Chapter 1: The Essence of Sri Vidya: A Divine Feminine Path

> **"At its heart, Sri Vidya emphasizes perceiving the Divine spark within all beings."**

Sri Vidya

Sri Vidya is a Hindu tantric tradition that worships the goddess Tripura Sundari, who is considered to be the supreme manifestation of Shakti, the divine energy. The name "Sri Vidya" means "the knowledge of the auspicious one."

Sri Vidya is a complex tradition with a rich history. It is based on the Tantras, a class of ancient Hindu scriptures that deal with esoteric knowledge. The Tantras teach that the universe is created, sustained, and destroyed by the play of Shakti. There are two main schools of thought within Sri Vidya: Dvaita and Advaita.

Dvaita Sri Vidya

Dvaita Sri Vidya, also known as "Dualistic Sri Vidya," emphasizes the duality of existence. It teaches that there is a fundamental distinction between the individual soul (Atman) and the supreme soul (Brahman). The goal of Dvaita Sri Vidya is to achieve union with Brahman through the worship of Tripura Sundari.

Advaita Sri Vidya

Advaita Sri Vidya, also known as "Non-dualistic Sri Vidya," emphasizes the unity of existence. It teaches that the individual soul is ultimately identical with the supreme soul. The goal of Advaita Sri Vidya is to realize this identity through the worship of Tripura Sundari.

Distinction between Dvaita and Advaita Sri Vidya

The main distinction between Dvaita and Advaita Sri Vidya lies in their understanding of the relationship between the individual soul and the supreme soul. Dvaita Sri Vidya sees this relationship as one of duality, while Advait Sri Vidya sees it as one of unity.

Another distinction between Dvaita and Advaita Sri Vidya lies in their approach to the worship of Tripura Sundari. Dvaita Sri Vidya emphasizes the worship of Tripura Sundari as a separate deity, while Advaita Sri Vidya emphasizes the worship of Tripura Sundari as the manifestation of the supreme soul.

Sri Vidya: Unveiling the Divine Light Within

Sri Vidya is a profound spiritual path that unlocks the secrets of the universe. It delves into the nature of the supreme energy (Sri) and the hidden reality (Tattva) behind the physical world (Prakriti). This knowledge encompasses the processes of creation, sustenance, and dissolution. It also illuminates the divine consciousness (Chaitanya) and its essence (Tattva).

> **"The study of Sri Vidya yields benefits for everyone, irrespective of their Dvaita or Advaita perspective."**

Pure Knowledge, Not Ritual

Unlike some tantric practices, Sri Vidya emphasizes pure knowledge (Shuddha vidya) rather than external rituals. Though the form Tripura Sundari is worshipped, the term "Sri" transcends gender, signifying a universal truth, not a feminine concept (Stri vidya). Sri Vidya is an internal exploration, similar to Yoga, requiring no material objects.

The Inner Light of Chaitanya

Chaitanya, the supreme light or knowledge or consciousness, resides naturally within each being. This inner light manifests uniquely to different people, appearing as Ganesha, Krishna, Shiva, Devi, or other divine forms, depending on their inclinations.

Masculine and Feminine Energy

Shiva (Masculine) and Shakti (Feminine) represent the essential interplay of consciousness (Potential) and energy (Manifestation). Shiva, the static, is pure potential; Shakti, the dynamic, is the force that actualizes it. They are not literal genders but symbolic principles within everyone, vital for balance and creation. Their unified dance, like Ardhanarishvara, symbolizes the interconnectedness of stillness and action, leading to a complete understanding of self and the universe.

Overall

Sri Vidya is a rich and complex tradition with a lot to offer. It is a tradition that can help us to understand the nature of reality and our place in it.

Chapter 2: Lalita Sahasranama: A Thousand-name hymn dedicated to Goddess Lalita

> **"Lalita Sahasranama is a profound revelation of the Universal Energy's nature."**

Lalita Sahasranama: A Divine Revelation

The Lalita Sahasranama is a sacred Hindu scripture that consists of 1000 divine names dedicated to the Supreme Mother, Lalita Devi. It is a unique composition that offers profound insights into the nature, attributes, cosmic plays, and power of the Divine.

Divine Origin

Unlike many other scriptures, the Lalita Sahasranama is not attributed to any human author. It is believed to have been revealed by the Divine Mother herself through the medium of the Devatas, the celestial beings who preside over speech and inspire human expression.

> **"Through the divine articulation of the eight Vagdevis, revealed by Lord Hayagriva to Sage Agastya, Lalita Sahasranama emerges as a deeply thought-provoking and potent hymn, a must-read for everyone."**

Structure and Significance

The Lalita Sahasranama is divided into two primary sections:

Moola Grantha: The initial 111 names of the Lalita Sahasranama, contained within 40 verses, constitute the Moola Grantha, serving as the foundational text. This section provides a condensed yet comprehensive overview of the Divine Mother's essential attributes and qualities, acting as a distilled summary of her nature before the subsequent verses elaborate on specific aspects.

Commentary: The remaining 889 names/143 verses act as commentaries on the moola grantha, offering deeper explanations and interpretations. They delve into specific aspects of the Divine Mother's nature and cosmic plays.

The Essence of the Lalita Sahasranama

The Lalita Sahasranama offers a wealth of spiritual knowledge and insights, including:

The Divine Mother's Nature: It reveals the various aspects of the Divine Mother's personality, such as her compassion, power, wisdom, and grace.

Cosmic Plays: The scripture describes the Divine Mother's cosmic plays, or leelas, through which she maintains the creation and sustains the universe.

Advaita Philosophy: It provides insights into Advaita Vedanta, the non-dualistic philosophy that emphasizes the oneness of the individual soul (Atman) with the universal consciousness (Brahman).

Yoga and Devotion: The Lalita Sahasranama offers guidance on various yoga practices and devotional paths that can lead to spiritual liberation.

Overall

The Lalita Sahasranama is a sacred text that offers a profound exploration of the Divine Feminine and the nature of reality. It is a source of inspiration, guidance, and spiritual upliftment for devotees of the Divine Mother.

Part II
The Philosophy of Advaita Vedanta

Chapter 3: Aham Brahmasmi : The Core of Vedanta

Brahman and "Aham Brahmasmi": The Unity of Consciousness

> "Within Advaita Vedanta, "Aham Brahmasmi" is a profound realization, not a mere intellectual understanding. It's a state of being."

Brahman, the ultimate reality in Hinduism, is often described as the all-pervading, formless, and timeless existence that underlies the entire universe. It is the source of all creation and the goal of spiritual seekers.

"Aham Brahmasmi" is a powerful mantra from the Upanishads, which translates to "I am Brahman." This declaration is a profound statement of identity, asserting that the individual self (Atman) is not separate from the universal consciousness (Brahman).

The Connection Between Brahman and "Aham Brahmasmi"

The mantra "Aham Brahmasmi" encapsulates the core of Hindu philosophy: the unity of all existence. It suggests that the individual soul is not a distinct entity but is, in essence, identical to the cosmic consciousness. The mantra "Aham Brahmasmi" is a powerful affirmation that requires a deep spiritual practice to fully realize its meaning.

Liberation: The mantra points to the ultimate goal of spiritual life: liberation from the cycle of birth and death (Samsara). When one realizes their identity as Brahman, they transcend the limitations of the individual self and attain eternal freedom.

The Path to "Aham Brahmasmi"

While the mantra "Aham Brahmasmi" is a powerful affirmation, it is not achieved through mere intellectual understanding. It requires a deep spiritual practice, often involving:

Meditation: Regular meditation helps to quiet the mind and cultivate a sense of inner peace, which is essential for realizing one's true nature.

Yoga: Yoga practices, both physical and mental, can help to purify the body and mind, making them receptive to spiritual experiences.

Study of the Vedas and Upanishads: The Vedas and Upanishads, the ancient sacred texts of Hinduism, offer profound insights into the nature of Brahman and the path to self-realization.

Devotion: Devotion to deities or spiritual teachers can provide inspiration and guidance on the spiritual journey.

Aham Brahmasmi, a profound mantra asserting the oneness of the individual soul with the universal consciousness, has had a far-reaching impact throughout history. Its influence extends to spiritual leaders, philosophers, and cultural movements within India.

> **"Aham Brahmasmi: not thought, but woven through stillness, breath, ancient words, and heart's devotion."**

One notable figure significantly influenced by this mantra is Adi Shankara, a renowned philosopher and proponent of Advaita Vedanta. Shankara's interpretations and teachings on non-duality, emphasizing the unity of the individual soul (Atman) with the universal consciousness (Brahman), have been instrumental in shaping the understanding and dissemination of the Aham Brahmasmi mantra.

Who am I?

This is one of the most thought provoking question a person have in his/her lifetime. Adi Shankara answered this question in his popular six-stanza prayer known as Atmashatkma or Nirvanashatkam. "Nirvana" means formless and "shatkam" refers to the 6 verses of the composition, expressing how the true Self is beyond all definitions; it is "neither this nor that". It was written around 9th Century CE. The essence of the prayer is : I am not body, I am God within. I am the Atman, the immortal soul, which is indeed GOD - Generator, Operator, Dissolver.

> **"Adi Shankara, a key proponent of Advaita Vedanta, emphasized the importance of realizing "Aham Brahmasmi" through discrimination and self-inquiry. He taught that true knowledge lies in recognizing this oneness. It signifies the removal of the illusion of separation between the self and the divine."**

Nirvana Shatkam

> **Mano buddhya ahammkāra cittāni nāham**
> **na ca śrotrajihve na ca ghrāṇanetre na**
> **ca vyoma bhūmir na tejo na vāyuḥ**
> **cidānanda rūpaḥ śivo'ham śivo'ham (1)**

I am not the mind, intellect, ego, or memory; neither the ears, tongue, nose, or eyes; nor ether, earth, fire, or air. I am the form of consciousness and bliss. I am Shiva! I am Shiva!

> **na ca praṇasajñona vai paṃcavāyuḥ**
> **na vā saptadhātur na vā paṃcakośaḥ na**
> **vākpāṇipādaṃ na copasthapāyu**
> **cidānandarūpaḥ śivo'ham śivo'ham (2)**

I am not the vital breath, nor the five vital airs; nor the seven bodily tissues, nor the five sheaths; nor the organs of speech, hands, feet, or procreation. I am the form of consciousness and bliss. I am Shiva! I am Shiva!

> na me dveṣarāgau na me lobhamohau
> madonaiva me naivamātsaryabhāvaḥ
> na dharmo na cārtho na kāmo na mokṣaḥ
> cidānandarūpaḥ śivo'ham śivo'ham (3)

I have neither aversion nor attachment, neither greed nor delusion; neither pride nor jealousy. I am not bound by dharma, artha, kama, or moksha. I am the form of consciousness and bliss. I am Shiva! I am Shiva!

> na puṇyaṃ na pāpaṃ na saukhyaṃ na dukhyaṃ
> na mantro na tīrthaṃ na vedā na yajña
> ahaṃ bhojanaṃ naiva bhojyaṃ na bhoktā
> cidānandarūpaḥ śivo'ham śivo'ham (4)

I am neither virtue nor vice, neither pleasure nor pain; neither mantra nor pilgrimage, neither Vedas nor sacrifices. I am neither the experiencer, the experience, nor the object of experience. I am the form of consciousness and bliss. I am Shiva! I am Shiva!

> na me mṛtyuśaṃkā na me jātibhedaḥ
> pitā naiva me naiva mātā na janmaḥ na
> bandhur na mitraṃ gurunaiva śiṣyaḥ
> cidānandarūpaḥ śivo'ham śivo'ham (5)

I have neither death nor fear, nor caste distinctions; neither father nor mother, nor birth. I have neither relatives nor friends, neither guru nor disciple. I am the form of consciousness and bliss. I am Shiva! I am Shiva!

> Ahaṃ nirvikalpo nirākāra rūpo
> vibhutvāca sarvatra sarveṃdriyāṇaṃ
> sada me samatvam na muktir na bandhaḥ
> cidānandarūpaḥ śivo'ham śivo'ham (6)

I am beyond all duality, formless, and all-pervading; I am everywhere, in all senses. I am neither attached, nor free, nor measurable. I am the form of consciousness and bliss. I am Shiva! I am Shiva!

Chapter 4: The Significance of Idol Worship: A Divine Symbolism

> "Ancient Hindu Rishis possessed a deep understanding of the natural world, acquired through keen observation and systematic inquiry, akin to the methods of early scientists."

The Power of Murti Puja

Hindu temple rituals and the practice of worshipping statues (Murti puja) are powerful ways to connect with the divine spirit within ourselves. For many, focusing on a specific image helps them concentrate and contemplate a particular aspect of God, rather than worshipping the physical object itself.

Beyond the Statue

While a statue may be a physical object, it represents a deeper spiritual truth. It's not the clay itself that we worship, but the divine essence it symbolizes. We all seek, whether we realize it or not, the ultimate reality that lies beyond the surface of our world. Every aspect of a statue, from its pose and hand gestures to its adornments and weapons, carries symbolic significance. After creation, the statue undergoes a sacred ritual that transforms it into a channel for divine energy. It becomes a source of positive vibration, connecting us to a higher power.

The Infinite and the Finite

The abstract nature of ultimate reality (Brahman, Emptiness, Universal Energy) makes it inherently difficult to grasp. While imposing a single, abstract concept would stifle the beauty of religious diversity, the core truth is that God is One, and we are all part of that singular life. Images act as essential tools, allowing us to connect with this vast, infinite reality through our senses.

> "Infinite reality, sensed through form, unified in essence."

The Hindu Perspective

Hindus knows Brahman transcends all concepts and images. This is why Hinduism has so many gods and goddesses. If the infinite cannot be perfectly expressed, there's no limit to the forms and names we can use to connect with it, depending on our individual inclination.

Diversity and Tolerance

This allows for the peaceful coexistence of diverse Hindu sects, each with their preferred deities. There's no competition over whose god is "best," but rather a deep acceptance of different paths to the divine.

The Personal Connection

> "Murti Puja is a heart's conversation with the divine, using an image as the meeting point. It is not idol worship, but a way to focus our love and connect to the formless through a form we can see and touch. A simple image, through faith, becomes a power source of divine energy."

Image worship allows us to connect with the divine on an emotional and personal level. We can interact with the image as if it were a beloved friend, expressing love, frustration, and gratitude. Just like we yearn to see and connect with those we love, so too do we seek a connection with the divine, become one with the Divine as we are the spark of that unique life (SOUL), miniature of the Universe. The Divine resides in all of us. As humans are sensory beings, images help us to connect with something beyond our physical world. These images are a "veil", allowing us to experience the divine in a way that nourishes our souls. Gradually, when one grows in spirituality, they shift their focus from outer worship to inner worship.

Chapter 5: God is Supereme Immortal Power: Does God belong to any religion?

> "Religion, at its heart, is a search for meaning, a bridge between the seen and the unseen. It offers a framework for morality, a community for solace, and a path for personal growth. When practiced with compassion, it can be a powerful force for good in the world."

The Problem with Religious Exclusivity

Many religions claim to have a monopoly on truth, asserting that their God is the only true God and their scriptures the only authentic revelation. This belief often leads to criticism and condemnation of other faiths, fostering global conflicts and even wars.

> "Recognizing the universality of Truth, all religions should be honored, understanding that no one faith holds exclusive rights to the divine or salvation."

The Unity of Divine Consciousness

Despite apparent differences, the underlying principle of all religions is the belief in a higher power. This suggests a fundamental unity of divine consciousness. God, in reality, transcends all religious labels and forms.

The Limitations of Religious Institutions

Religions offer valuable guidance and structure, but their focus on specific beliefs and practices can inadvertently hinder spiritual growth. By defining God within strict boundaries, they may prevent individuals from experiencing a direct, personal connection with the divine and realizing their own inherent spiritual nature. This can create a conflict between the external framework of religion and the internal journey of self-discovery.

The Purpose of Religion

Religion serves as a foundation for spiritual exploration providing basic teachings and practices. However, it should not be the ultimate destination. As individuals mature spiritually, they should strive to transcend the limitations of religious dogma and experience a direct connection with the divine.

Beyond Religious Rituals

Many people blindly follow religious rituals without understanding their deeper meaning. This mechanical adherence can hinder spiritual progress. True spiritual growth requires a conscious effort to understand and experience the underlying principles of faith.

The Inner Kingdom of God

Despite the teachings of scriptures that emphasize the divine within, many continue to search for God externally. The Upanishads, foundational texts of Hinduism, offer a profound understanding of the divine nature of the individual soul.

The Unity of Soul and Divine

The Upanishads fundamentally assert the unity of the individual soul, Atman, with the universal Divine, Brahman, a profound truth conveyed through powerful statements. "Tat Tvam Asi" (Thou Art That), "Ayam Atma Brahma" (This Atman is Brahman), and "Prajnanam Brahma" (Consciousness is Brahman) serve as core affirmations of this non dualistic reality, emphasizing that the essence of the self is inseparable from the ultimate reality. These declarations encapsulate the central philosophy of the Upanishads, revealing the inherent divinity within each individual.

> **"True understanding of the divine requires transcending rigid religious doctrines and embracing direct spiritual experience through inner peace and heightened awareness."**

The Divine Presence Everywhere

The Upanishads emphasize the pervasiveness of the Divine. The statement "Aham Brahmasmi" (I am Brahman) asserts the divine nature of every individual, recognizing that each person is a manifestation of the Supreme Immortal Power.

The Divine Spark Within

Every scripture acknowledges the divine spark within each individual. The Upanishads, in particular, provide a profound and comprehensive understanding of this truth, offering guidance for those seeking to realize their divine nature.

Oral Tradition and Sacred Texts

For countless generations, the scriptures have been orally transmitted through song and poetry, eventually being written down. The universe's profound secrets are concealed in the coded language of these ancient texts.

> "The tradition now known as Hinduism was originally referred to as Sanatana Dharma, meaning 'Eternal Righteousness.' The term 'Hinduism' was later introduced by Persians in the 6th century BCE, who used it to describe the people and practices of the Indus River region."

Part III
Unveiling the Divine Within - AHAM BRAHMASMI

Chapter 6: Verses 1-23: The Divine Feminine Unveiled

> "These 23 verses are not aimed at external worship, but rather at the profound realization of our own inherent divinity. These verses move beyond superficial beauty, declaring the cosmos itself as our ornament, where countless stars and planets mirror the vastness of our being."

INTRODUCTION TO VERSES 1 to 23

Verse 1 to 3

When we chant the first three verses of Lalita Sahasranama, Basically we aim at invoking the Divine Energy and these three verses depicts the functional nature of the Divine Universal Energy. The First Verse starts with "Sri Mata" - The Universal Mother.

Verse 4 to 23

Lalita is the joyful dynamic and sparkling expression of the Self. A free consciousness, well-founded in the Self. The Verses 4-23 delves into the interconnectedness of the human body, mind, senses and the universe, using captivating descriptions of the body and its flawless nature. It emphasizes that every part of our physical form works in perfect harmony, highlighting the wonder and complexity of existence. These verses transcends mere physical beauty by stating that the universe itself is our adornment, with countless stars and planets reflecting the grand scale of our existence. It emphasizes the concept of microcosm and macrocosm - that we, as individuals, are miniature reflections of the vast cosmos.

VERSE 1 - Names 1 to 5

Śhrī-mātā,Śhrī-mahā-rājñī,Śhrī-mat-siṁh'āsan'eśhvarī,
Chid-agni-kuṇḍa-sambhūtā,Deva-kārya-samudyatā.

Glory! Sacred Mother, Great Empress, Supreme Goddess of
the Lion-throne; Born out of the sacred fire-pit of
consciousness, You emerge for a Divine purpose.

Śhrī-mātā - The Universal Mother

Śhrī - Title of Respect, Greatest; Mātā - mother

Śhrī-mahā-rājñī - The Supereme Queen

Śhrī -Title of Respect, Greatest; Mahā - Vast, Rājñī - Queen; Mahā-rājñī - Queen of queens

Śhrī-mat-siṁh'āsan'eśhvarī - Seated on a Lion Throne

Śhrī-mat - This is an extension of 1st Name - Supreme respect given to her in her capacity; Siṁha - Lion; Āsana - Seat; Īśhvarī - Ruler

Chid-agni-kuṇḍa-sambhūtā - Born from the Fire Altar of Consciousness

Cit - consciousness/awareness; Agni-kuṇḍa - Fire Altar; Sambhuta - Born

Deva-kārya-samudyatā - Engaged in the Work of the Devas

Deva - Devas (Gods and Goddesses); Kārya - Work, Task; Samudyatā - Offer/ Engaged in

The Language of Love: Motherhood in the Lalita Sahasranama

Just like a child instinctively seeks their mother in moments of joy and hardship, the Lalita Sahasranama begins with the most fundamental expression of love - Śhrī-mātā, the Divine Mother. She represents the universal maternal force, the source of all physical and intangible creation.

The Threefold Mother: Creation, Preservation and Dissolution

The first two names in the Lalita Sahasranama highlight two essential aspects of motherhood: creation and sustenance. Śrī-mātā embodies the creative power, while the following name emphasizes her ability to nurture and sustain all existence.

The Divine Mother is often depicted seated upon a lion, a powerful symbol often associated with both fierceness and dissolution. This seemingly contradictory image can be understood through the lens of motherhood.

One interpretation sees the lion as a representation of the supreme queen, powerful enough to sustain the universe. Another interpretation views the lion as the devotee, fearless, and ready for transformation. This transformation, like a dissolving ego, is a necessary step on the path to enlightenment.

Beyond Form: Waking the Divine Within

The name "Chid-agni-kuṇḍa-sambhūtā" delves into a deeper level of meaning. "Cit" refers to pure consciousness, and "Agni kunda" symbolizes the fire altar within each person (Mooladhara Chakra). Rather than a literal birth from fire, this name signifies the awakening of Kundalini, the divine energy within the devotee. This awakening eliminates negative tendencies and cultivates divine qualities.

Dispelling Darkness, Guiding the Way

The Lalita Sahasranama portrays the Divine Mother as the ultimate source of consciousness. She dispels ignorance, illuminating the path within and clearing away the darkness of illusion.

> "Mother's fierce love: creating, sustaining, dissolving illusion, awakening the divine within."

A Universal Benefactress

The Divine Mother's compassion extends to all beings. She empowers the devas (divine beings) in their struggles and guides humans (jivas) towards virtuous actions and knowledge of the ultimate reality (Brahman).

Thought - provoking prompt
Esoteric Meaning - VERSE 1

Within each of us lies a potent force of divine energy called Kundalini Shakti. Unlike a dormant spark, it's a wellspring of energy that flows at different levels for everyone. Through meditation, we can cultivate awareness and gently awaken this powerful force within.

Kundalini Shakti is formless, residing within us. When we connect with it through mindful meditation, it elevates our consciousness and sets a wave of universal energy in motion towards our intentions which creates, sustains, destroy and enables us to carry virtuous actions. This awakened Shakti, fearless and potent, can be seen as the conductor of the universe, directing our inner light outward.

VERSE 2 - Names 6 to 9

> Udyad-bhānu-sahasrābhā,Chatur-bāhu-samanvitā,
> Rāga-swarūpa-paśh'āḍhyā,Krodh'ākār'ānkuśh'ojjvalā.
>
> Glory! Shining like a thousand rising suns, You are endowed with four arms; Holding a noose as the form of passions, blazing with a goad as the form of anger.

Udyad-bhānu-sahasrābhā - The one who shines with the radiant of a thousand rising suns
Udyad - Rising; Bhānu - Sun, Sahasra - Thousand; Ābhā - Light

Chatur-bāhu-samanvitā - The one who has four arms
Chatur - Four; Bāhu - Arms; Samanvitā - Possessing

Rāga-swarūpa-paśh'āḍhyā - The one who holds the ropes of desires
Rāga - Desires; Rāga-swarūpa - In the form of desires; Paśh'āḍhyā -Rope

Krodh'ākār'ānkuśh'ojjvalā - The one who shines with the goad of anger
Krodh - Anger; Ākāra - Knowledge; Ānkuśh - Arrow to mean control; Jvalā - Light

Lalitambika: Dazzling Radiance and Powerful Arms

Lalitambika's brilliance surpasses that of a thousand suns rising in unison. The Sahasrara chakra, the seventh and highest energy center within us, is said to have a thousand petals, each radiating with the fiery glow. When this magnificent lotus fully blooms, it reflects the light of a thousand suns – a fitting depiction of Lalitambika's resplendent form. It represents the unlimited potential.

> "A thousand suns blooming within, limitless potential revealed."

Red: The Color of Love and Protection

Consistent with ancient scriptures and tantric texts, Lalitambika is traditionally portrayed with a red complexion. This color symbolizes not just the rising sun but also the profound care and affection a mother showers upon her children. It represents her unwavering presence, watching over her devotees with love and protection.

Four Arms: Instruments of Upliftment

Lalitambika's four arms are not simply physical; they are potent instruments of grace, designed to guide and elevate her followers. This verse details the objects held in two of her arms, with the remaining two described in the subsequent verse. Each arm bears a distinct symbolic implement.

Pasa (Noose): Held in her left hand, the Pasa represents a rope. This name signifies Lalita Devi's control over desires and shows the right path. She is the one who helps us to fulfill our desires. She showers her love on us.

Elephant Hook: Lalitambika's right hand holds an elephant hook, a potent symbol of her ability to break through the destructive force of hatred within her devotees. This divine tool signifies her power to transform anger into positive, constructive energy, guiding individuals towards forgiveness and the recognition of the inherent divine spark within each being. By wielding the elephant hook, she helps us transcend negative emotions, fostering a deeper understanding of universal connection and enabling us to use our energy for benevolent purposes.

**Thought - provoking prompt
Esoteric Meaning - VERSE 2**

The second verse of the Lalita Sahasranama illuminates the multifaceted nature of Divine Energy, likened to 'a thousand rising suns' to convey its boundless power. This universal energy, driven by benevolence, fulfills the desires of devoted hearts. Yet, it also wields the tools of discipline and transformation, symbolized by the interchangeable noose and goad, representing compassion alongside corrective action. This twofold aspect extends to fostering forgiveness; just as the goad guides, it also prompts self-reflection, allowing devotees to release grudges and embrace the transformative power of divine grace, recognizing that corrective action often paves the way for deeper understanding and reconciliation.

VERSE 3 - Names 10 to 12

> Mano-rūp'ekṣhu-kodaṇḍā,Pañcha-tanmātra-sāyakā,
> Nij'āruṇa-prabhā-pūra-majjad-brahmāṇḍa-maṇḍalā.
>
> Glory! Weilding a sugar-cane bow in the form of mind, and
> the five elements as arrows; You fill the whole Universe
> with Your own rose-tinted brilliance.

Mano-rūp'ekṣhu-kodaṇḍā - The one who holds the bow of the mind

Mano-rūp - In the form of mind; Ikṣhu - Sugarcane; Kodaṇḍā - Bow

Pañcha-tanmātra-sāyakā - The one who has the five arrows of the subtle elements

Pañcha - Five; Tanmātra - Essence or subtle attributes of five basic elements i.e., sound, sight, taste, smell, and touch (subtle modifications of the five basic elements - akash, air, fire, water, and earth); Sāyakā - Arrow

Nij'āruṇa-prabhā-pūra-majjad-brahmāṇḍa-maṇḍalā - The one who fills the universe with red - radiance

Nij'āruṇa - Constant Red; Prabhā - Radiance-Glow; Pūra - Complete; Majjad - Submerge; Brahmāṇḍa-maṇḍalā - Universal Territory

Weapons of Transformation: The Sugarcane Bow and Flower Arrows

The Cosmic Mind

The goddess is depicted holding a sugarcane bow in one of her left arms. This symbolizes the cosmic mind. The process of extracting sweet juice from sugarcane by crushing it mirrors the purification of the mind to unveil the sweetness of Brahman, the ultimate reality.

Flower Arrows: Playful Tools for Dispelling Illusion

In her other hand, the goddess holds five floral arrows crafted from Lotus, Raktakaivara, Kalhara, Indivara, and Mango flowers. These symbolize the potent emotions of excitement, madness, confusion, stimulation, and destruction respectively. However, these arrows are not weapons of harm but tools for the divine play - **LEELA**. They are used to pierce the illusions of devotees, guiding them towards liberation. This also refers to Lalita Devi's power over the five subtle elements (sound, touch, sight, taste, and smell). She is the one who helps us to transcend these elements and to experience the true nature of reality.

Red Radiance: A Universal Embrace

The goddess's radiant red complexion is symbolic of her universal care and compassion. As the mother of the cosmos, she nurtures all beings with her love.

This symbolic representation of the divine feminine encapsulates the complex interplay between the cosmic mind, the divine play, and unconditional maternal love.

Thought - provoking prompt
Esoteric Meaning - VERSE 3

Our perceptions of the world, shaped by our senses, fundamentally influence our thoughts and emotions. Love, compassion, and anger, among countless other feelings, are mental and sensual constructs. It's common knowledge that positive thoughts invite positivity, while negative ones attract negativity. However, our bodies have a finite capacity for enduring emotional turmoil. When this limit is exceeded, a cosmic force intervenes to realign our perspective, demonstrating its boundless love and care for all beings.

VERSE 4 - Names 13 and 14

> Champak'āshoka-punnāga-saugandhika-lasat-kachā,
> Kuruvinda-maṇi-śhreṇī-kanat-koṭīra-maṇḍitā.
>
> Glory! Your hair has a beautiful fragrance of Champaka,
> Ashoka and Punnaga flowers; And You are adorned with a
> crown of the finest rubies.

Champak'āshoka-punnāga-saugandhika-lasatkachā - The
one whose hair is adorned with Champaka, Ashoka,
Punnaga and Saughandhika Flowers
Champak'āshoka-punnāga-saugandhika - Types of fragrant
flowers; Lasat - Shiny; Kacha - Hair

Kuruvinda-maṇi-śhreṇī-kanat-koṭīra-maṇḍitā - The one who
is adorned with a string of Kuruvinda rubies on the crown of
her head
Kuruvinda-maṇi - Kuruvinda is a rare type of ruby; Sreni -
String; Kanat - Shine; Mandita - Stays decorated

The Fragrance of Divinity

Champak, Ashoka, Punnga, and Saugandhika flowers adorn her
hair, yet their fragrance is not their own. Instead, it emanates
from the divine essence within her. These four blooms symbolize
the deceptive nature of the mind, intellect, consciousness, and
ego.

The Yogi's Aura

Spiritual adepts are known for their pleasant bodily aroma, a
result of balanced bodily humors rather than external perfumes.
The true fragrance is not in the flower, but in the divinity that
blooms within.

The Ruby of Devotion

The Kuruvinda, a rare red ruby, represents love, prosperity, and devotion. Meditating on her adorned with such a gem is believed to deepen one's spiritual connection.

Thought - provoking prompt
Esoteric Meaning - VERSE 4

Verses 4-23 shift the focus from external idol worship to internal self-realization. The concept of a "sweet-smelling state" refers to the elevated vibrational frequency of meditators, characterized by an abundance of positive energy. People are naturally drawn to those emitting such high vibrations. By invoking divine energy, individuals undergo a transformative process, elevating their being to a higher vibrational plane. Every part of their body resonates at a higher frequency. The "Kuruvinda" ruby, symbolizing love, prosperity, and devotion, is linked to the crown chakra (Sahasrara). Meditating on this Chakra is believed to enhance devotion towards Divine, bring prosperity and enhance self-love, love for others and spiritual growth.

VERSE 5 - Names 15 and 16

> Aṣhṭamī-chandra-vibhrāja-dalika-sthala-śhobhitā,
> Mukha-chandra-kalaṅkābha-mṛiga-nābhi-viśheṣhakā.
>
> Glory! Your forehead is resplendent like the half-moon on the eighth day; And Your musk tilak is a dark spot on the face of the moon.

Aṣhṭamī-chandra-vibhrāja-dalika-sthala-śhobhitā - The one whose forehead shines beautifully like the moon on the eighth day.
Aṣhṭamī-chandra - Eighth day from the full moon or new moon is called as Ashtmi/Crescent Moon on the eighth day from full moon; Vibhrāja - To shine across; Dalika - Forehead; Sthala - Section; Śhobhitā - Beautiful, Resplendent

Mukha-chandra-kalaṅkābha-mṛiga-nābhi-viśheṣhakā - The one whose face is like the moon, marked with the musky scent of a deer.
Mukha-chandra - Face which is like moon; Kalaṅkābha - Blemish/Mark/Spot; Mṛiga-nābhi - Musk (From Deer); Viśheṣhakā - Peculiar

The Moon as a Metaphor and Mental Balance

The forehead of Lalita Devi is compared with the moon on the eighth day of fortnight. The moon looks similar on both days of both bright and dark fortnights. This symbolism mirrors the cyclical nature of human experience. In Indian tradition, the moon symbolizes the mind. The verse suggests the importance of maintaining mental equilibrium regardless of life's ups and downs.

> "Lalita's moon-forehead, a mirrored mind's calm, Where cycles turn, and earthly stains find balm."

Divine Adornment and Tantric Practice

The "stain on the moon" represents imperfections that can obscure mental clarity. Musk, a traditionally used beauty product, holds significance in Tantric rituals when applied to the forehead. This contrast between celestial purity and earthly adornment adds depth to the imagery.

Thought - provoking prompt
Esoteric Meaning - VERSE 5

The fifth verse of the Lalita Sahasranama offers profound wisdom on navigating life's up's and downs. It posits that a serene and equanimous mind is the ultimate armor against life's storms. The verse subtly alludes to the mercurial nature of the mind, prone to fluctuations. As a reminder to counterbalance, the ancient tradition of ritual, metaphorically represented by musk, is introduced. This practice, served as a steadfast anchor, grounding the mind and shielding it from the stormy waves of unwanted thoughts.

VERSE 6 - Names 17 and 18

> Vadana-smara-māṅgalya-gṛiha-toraṇa-chillikā,
> Vaktra-lakshmi-parīvāha-chalan-mīn'ābha-lochanā.
>
> Glory! The eyebrows in Your smiling face are the arches to
> the wedding palace of Cupid; And Your eyes are like
> darting fishes in the ocean of beauty of Your face.

Vadana-smara-māṅgalya-gṛiha-toraṇa-chillikā - The one
whose face is like the glorious palace of the Cupid (The God
of Love) and her eyebrows are the entrance arches of that
palace.
Vadana - Face; Smara - When reflecting; Māṅgalya - Auspicious;
Gṛiha - House; Toraṇa - Doorway; Chillikā - Eyebrow

Vaktra-lakshmi-parīvāha-chalan-mīn'ābha-lochanā - The
one whose eyes are like the moving fish, resembling the
procession of the goddess of wealth.
Vaktra - Face; Parīvāha - Channel of Water/ Pool; Lakshmi-parīvāha -
Channel of Water which Lakshmi calls her own; Chalan -Moving;
Mīna - Fish; Ābha - Shining; Lochanā - Eyes

Divine Beauty

Lalita Devi's beauty is unparalleled. Her eyebrows, likened to
ornate portals, invite souls to a heavenly realm. Her face, a
celestial palace, is adorned with these exquisite arches. Her eyes,
constantly moving like fish, protect and nurture creation.

Divine Grace

Lalita Devi's gaze is a source of immense power. Her
compassionate look is believed to bestow the grace of Lakshmi,
a blessing often misunderstood as mere wealth. In reality, this
divine grace encompasses spiritual riches, occult powers, and

divine qualities. By her mercy, devotees receive abundance in both material and spiritual realms.

**Thought - provoking prompt
Esoteric Meaning - VERSE 6**

The verse implies that those deeply connected to the divine - adepts, devotees, or anyone invoking divine energy are often characterized by their immense love for others and a constant state of happiness. Their faces radiate with joy and kindness. In contrast, people burdened by frustration typically wear their emotions on their sleeves, with frowns reflecting their inner turmoil. Our perspective on the world is shaped by our own emotional lens, through which we view reality. Humans are creatures of desire, and when we focus on our goals with love and determination, divine energy is believed to assist in their manifestation. The description of her eyes as being like moving fish can be interpreted as a reminder that we should appreciate the beauty of life and also to incorporate focused attention and visualization to achieve goals in life which bestows riches.

VERSE 7 - Names 19 and 20

**Nava-champaka-puṣhpābha-nāsā-ḍaṇḍa-virājitā,
Tārā-kānti-tiras-kāri- nāsā-bharaṇa-bhāsurā.**

**Glory! Your nose is like a newly opened Champaka
blossom; And the brilliance of Your diamond nose-ring
puts the stars to shame.**

**Nava-champaka-puṣhpābha-nāsā-ḍaṇḍa-virājitā - The one
whose nose is like a new Champaka Flower, adorned with a
nose stud.**
Nava - New; Champaka - Champaka Flower; Puṣhpa - Flower; Ābha -
Radiant; Nāsā - Nose; Dhanda - Authority; Virājitā - Present

**Tārā-kānti-tiras-kāri-nāsā-bharaṇa-bhāsurā - Whose nose
instrument is brighter than the stars, which is a symbol of
her power and radiance.**
Tārā - Stars; Kānti-Brightness; Tiras-kāri - Outshines/Excel; Nasa -
Nose; Bharaṇa - Bearing; Bhāsurā - Shining

The Divine Fragrance of Purity

Lalita Devi's nose is poetically compared to a freshly bloomed
Champaka flower, exuding purity and fragrance. This
comparison extends beyond physical beauty. The nose, the
gateway to life-sustaining breath, mirrors the soul's intake of
spiritual essence. Just as we instinctively recoil from unpleasant
odors, we should shun negative influences to nurture our
spiritual well-being. This aligns with meditative practices that
focus on inhaling positivity and exhaling negativity.

Celestial Beauty and Divine Power

Devi's nose stud is a dazzling ornament that eclipses the
brilliance of celestial bodies. Its diamond radiance surpasses that
of stars and planets, represented by the term Tara. This divine

adornment not only signifies unparalleled beauty but also implies a power that transcends cosmic forces.

Thought - provoking prompt
Esoteric Meaning - VERSE 7

The comparison of Lalita Devi's nose to a Champaka bud carries deep esoteric significance. The nose is not merely a physical organ but a symbolic gateway. In spiritual tradition, the breath is considered the bridge between the physical and spiritual realms. In the spirit of meditation, this practice seeks to cleanse the mind by inhaling light (positivity) and exhaling darkness (negativity). The Champaka, known for its intoxicating fragrance, represents divine consciousness or pure awareness. Thus, the nose becomes a conduit for the inhalation of spiritual essence. This is akin to yogic practices where the breath is used to focus the mind and cleanse the Aura. Also, the emphasis on good and bad actions aligns with the concept of karma. By choosing virtuous paths, one is essentially purifying through spiritual intake.

The nose stud, outshining celestial bodies, suggests the ability of breath to connect higher realms. Its brilliance suggests a direct connection to the divine light. It's a poetic description of the spiritual journey, hinting at the possibility of human divinity.

VERSE 8 - Names 21 and 22

> **Kadamba-mañjari-klṛipta-karṇa-pūra-manoharā,
> Tāṭanka-yugalī-bhūta-tapan-oḍupa-maṇḍalā.**
>
> **Glory! The adornment of Kadamba flowers all around Your ears makes You fascinating; With the orbs of the sun and moon as Your ear-rings.**

Kadamba-mañjari-klṛipta-karṇa-pūra-manoharā - The one whose ears are adorned with clusters of Kadamba flowers, which are more charming than the moon
Kadamba - Kadamba Flower; Mañjari - A Cluster of Blossom; Klṛipta - Arranged; Karṇa-pūra - Ornament worn around the ears; Manoharā - Enchanting

Tāṭanka-yugalī-bhūta-tapan-oḍupa-maṇḍalā - The one whose earrings are made of sun and moon discs
Tāṭanka - Ear stud/ Ear Rings; Yugalī - Wearing a Pair; Bhūta -Present; Tapan - Sun; Uḍupa - Moon; Maṇḍalā - Globe/Halo around the Sun and the Moon

The Kadamba and Divine Environment

A Kadamba manjari is a cluster of Kadamba blossoms. Lalita Devi is often depicted adorned with these fragrant flowers behind her ears. The divine scent of these flowers is believed to emanate from her own aura. She is aptly named Kadamba Vana Vasini, the dweller in the Kadamba forest, indicating her affinity for this sacred tree. This imagery suggests a profound truth: surrounding oneself with positive influences can create a harmonious and peaceful environment. It also symbolises the effects of divine chants in our life.

Celestial Adornment and Tantric Symbolism

The sun and moon grace Lalita Devi's ears, symbolizing her cosmic control. These celestial bodies sustain life, mirroring the goddess's life-giving energy. This description unveils a deeper tantric interpretation. Lalita Devi represents the Sushumna nadi as Kundalini moves through Sushumna nadi, the central energy channel. The Ida and Pingala nadis, associated with the moon and sun respectively, flank this central channel. This poetic portrayal hints at the esoteric practice of Kundalini awakening, where balancing these energy channels leads to spiritual illumination and union with the divine.

Thought - provoking prompt
Esoteric Meaning - VERSE 8

The passage offers a symbolic representation of the spiritual journey. The Kadamba flower symbolizes the divine environment that fuels spirituality, while the goddess adorned with the sun and moon represents the ultimate goal of spiritual practice - the union of individual consciousness with the cosmic consciousness. The imagery of the energy channels implies the path to this union, suggesting that by harmonizing the inner energies, various yogic practices, one can attain divine consciousness. It also hints that we should pay attention to the divine chants, positive opinions and reject negative opinions of others.

VERSE 9 - Names 23 and 24

> **Padma-rāga-śhil'ādarśha-pari-bhāvi-kapola-bhūḥ,**
> **Nava-vidruma-bimba-śhrī-nyak-kāri-radanach-chhadā.**
>
> **Glory! Your cheeks surpass the beauty of mirrors made of rubies; And Your delicate lips humble the shining beauty of fresh coral or Bimba fruit.**

Padma-rāga-śhil'ādarśha-pari-bhāvi-kapola-bhūḥ - The one whose cheeks surpass the beauty of mirrors made of rubies
Padma-rāga - A type of ruby which is red in colour; Śhila - Stone (Here Gemstone); Darśha - View/Be seen; Pari-bhāvi -Visualised/Imagined ; Kapola - Cheek; Bhūḥ - Being, The Earth

Nava-vidruma-bimba-śhrī-nyak-kāri-radanach-chhadā - The one with delicate lips that make as nothing the shining beauty of fresh coral or Bimba fruit
Nava - Fresh; Vidruma - Coral; Bimba - When compared; Śhrī -Here means lusture or radiance; Nyak-kāri - To degrade; Radanach-chhadā - Lip(s)

The Symbolism of Red and the power of Meditation

Red, a color synonymous with life and love, is prominently featured in the description of Lalita Devi. Her cheeks, known as kapōla, are likened to the vibrant hue of a rose. This rosy complexion is believed to be a source of vitality and affection. It represents love and happiness. Devotees are encouraged to meditate on the intense red color of Lalita Devi's cheeks. This focused contemplation is thought to enhance one's own liveliness and enthusiasm.

The Allure of Her Lips

Lalita Devi's lips are described as surpassing the beauty of the bimba fruit, both renowned for their rich red color. Meditating on the captivating crimson of her lips is believed to imbue the devotee's speech with a similar enchanting quality.

Thought - provoking prompt
Esoteric Meaning - VERSE 9

Love is often equated with happiness, and this sentiment is reflected on the human face. Our cheeks, mirrors of our emotional landscape, blush with a rosy hue when we experience emotional well-being. This vibrant color embodies joy, affection, compassion, and mental clarity. Similarly, our lips, instruments of expression and creation, carry the potential for manifestation when imbued with the energy of red. By focusing on these, we can cultivate inner strength, emotional equilibrium, and the ability to create positive realities. Ultimately, this passage suggests that our thoughts, feelings, and speech collectively shape our experiences and destinies.

VERSE 10 - Names 25 and 26

Śhuddha-vidy'ānkur-ākāra-dvija-pankti-dvay'ojjvalā,
Karpūra-vītikā-moda-samākarṣhi-digantarā.

Glory! Your shining teeth are two rows of sprouts of the Pure Knowledge; The Betel leaves and camphor that You chew, make the whole Universe fragrant.

Śhuddha-vidy'ānkur-ākāra-dvija-pankti-dvay'ojjvalā - The one whose two gleamimg rows of teeth are fresh sprouts of the pure knowledge
Śhuddha - Pure; Vidya - Knowledge; Ānkura - Sprouts, Shoots; Ākāra - To appear/ Appearance; Dvija - Teeth (Twice born); Pankti - Row or Arrangement; Dvaya - Two, Pair; Ujjvalā - Shine

Karpūra-vītikā-moda-samākarṣhi-digantarā - The one whose breath is fragrant like camphor attracting all directions
Karpūra - Camphor; Vītikā - Variety of Spices and nuts chewed along with betel leaves; Moda - Fragrance; Samākarṣhi - Far Spreading Aroma; Digantarā - Space

The Teeth as Divine Symbols

Lalita Devi's teeth are likened to Shuddha Vidya, the supreme form of worship for the Divine Mother. This powerful knowledge is associated with a sixteen-syllabled mantra. Her thirty-two teeth, then, represent two rows of these sacred sound seeds or bija mantras. This symbolism is enhanced by the Sanskrit word dvija, meaning 'twice-born' or 'initiated,' which also refers to those enlightened through the mantra's power. By contemplating her teeth as these divine sounds, devotees can dissolve deep-rooted mental impressions or samskaras, liberating themselves from karmic bondage and attaining a state of transcendent consciousness.

"Karma dissolved by sacred sound, ignorance lured by fragrant ground."

The Breath of Divinity

The comparison of Lalita Devi's breath to camphor is profound. Like camphor that evaporates without residue, leaving behind a pure fragrance, the Divine Mother transcends the three qualities of nature (rajas, tamas, and sattva). Her divine essence then fills the devotee with a sacred aura. This fragrance, however, serves a dual purpose - it attracts both the spiritually inclined and the ignorant. While the former are drawn to her through devotion, the latter require this alluring scent as a catalyst for spiritual awakening.

Thought - provoking prompt
Esoteric Meaning - VERSE 10

The description of Lalita Devi's teeth as Shuddha Vidya carries deep esoteric implications. Teeth, in esoteric traditions, are often linked to the power of speech and manifestation. It represents that our words have a great influence on what we manifest.

Shuddha Vidya itself implies pure knowledge or consciousness. Thus, Lalita Devi's teeth represent the manifestation of divine consciousness in sound form. Meditating on these teeth is akin to immersing oneself in the primordial cosmic vibration, leading to a direct experience of the divine. This also hints that we attain knowledge from our teachers, gurus, mentors. That knowledge is divine knowledge and should be respected. We are also embodiment of the knowledge. When we turn our attention inwards and meditate, we receive divine guidance. The annihilation of samskaras through this meditation indicates a purification of consciousness. Just as teeth break down food, the mantra (knowledge), represented by the teeth, breaks down the mental impurities, paving the way for spiritual enlightenment.

Lalita Devi's breath, likened to camphor, suggests that her very essence is transformative. It dissolves the three gunas (qualities of nature) in the devotee, leading to a state of pure consciousness. The fragrance emanating from the camphor can be interpreted as the divine grace that spreads to all beings.

VERSE 11 - Names 27 and 28

Nija-sallāpa-mādhurya-vinir-bhartsita-kachchhapī,
Manda-smita-prabhāpūra-majjat-kāmeśha-mānasā.

Glory! The sweetness of Your discourse puts to shame the Veena of Śhrī Saraswati; And into the stream of Your entrancing smile the mind of Śhrī Siva is drowned.

Nija-sallāpa-mādhurya-vinir-bhartsita-kachchhapī - The sweetness of whose discourse puts to shame the Veena of Saraswati

Nija - Personal; Sallāpa - Conversation; Mādhurya - Sweetness; Vinir-bhartsita - Put to shame; Kachchhapī - Veena Instrument

Manda-smita-prabhāpūra-majjat-kāmeśha-mānasā - The one into whose gentle and entrancing smile the mind of Shiva is drowned

Manda - Gentle; Smita - Smile; Prabhā - Splendour; Pūra - Full of; Majjat - Essence; Kāmeśha - Lord Shiva; Mānasā - Mind

The Enchanting Power of Speech

Lalita Devi's speech is likened to the melodious music produced by Saraswati Devi's kachchhapī (a type of lute). This comparison highlights the enchanting quality of her words. The underlying message is the importance of pure and kind speech, which has the power to uplift and inspire.

The Irresistible Power of Divine Grace

Lalita Devi's smile is described as captivating even Lord Shiva, the conqueror of love. This imagery underscores the irresistible power of divine grace. The subtle meaning suggests that when individuals reach a point of despair or exhaustion, surrendering to a higher power can be transformative. It implies that divine intervention is often sought as a last resort when human

---

resilience reaches its limit. It also signifies that the power of smile of the person to attract people, experiences and positive outcomes.

Thought - provoking prompt
Esoteric Meaning - VERSE 11

This passage highlights the profound influence of spoken words. When chosen and delivered with care, words can exert a magnetic pull, drawing others in. This influence is particularly strong with those who possess a high level of positive energy, often referred to as high vibrations. These individuals radiate an attractive force that not only uplifts those around them but also has the potential to transform even the most hardened hearts. It's as if, when negativity reaches its peak, a wellspring of inner divinity erupts, triggering a positive transformation. Similarly, a radiant smile can have a magnetic effect, attracting others and bringing about positive change in their lives. The gentle and enchanting smile is a symbol of positive emotion, capable of raising our vibrational frequency and attracting positive experiences and outcomes.

VERSE 12 - Names 29 and 30

> **Anākalita-sādṛiśhya-chibuka-śhrī-virājitā,**
> **Kāmeśha-baddha-māṅgalya-sūtra-śhobhita-kandharā.**
>
> **Glory! Your chin is a splendid adornment which has no comparison; And beautifying Your neck is the Mangala-sutra tied by Śhrī Śhiva Himself.**

Anākalita-sādṛiśhya-chibuka-śhrī-virājitā - The one who is adorned with a chin the likeness of whose splendour has never been seen
Anākalita - Unobserved; Sādṛiśhya - Resemblence; Chibuka - Chin; Śhrī - Auspicious; Virājitā - Adorned

Kāmeśha-baddha-māṅgalya-sūtra-śhobhita-kandharā - The one who is beautified by the wedding necklace around the neck tied by Śhrī Śhiva Himself
Kāmeśha - Lord Shiva; Baddha - Tied; Māṅgalya-sūtra -Wedding Necklace; Śhobhita - Beautiful; Kandharā - Neck

The Beauty of Lalita Devi's Chin

Lalita Devi's chin, aptly named Chibuka, is renowned for its exquisite beauty. This facial feature holds significance beyond aesthetics, as it is considered a representation of one's vital force in physiognomy. The more striking the chin, the more powerful the life energy. In the case of Lalita Devi, her chin's beauty is a reflection of her extraordinary vitality.

The Symbolic Significance of the Mangalya Sutura

Adorning Lalita Devi's neck is the Mangalya Sutura, a sacred necklace worn by married Hindu women. This ornament comprises two delicate golden circles embedded within a chain, a design that mirrors the rhythmic pattern of human breath – inhalation and exhalation. This duality of breath is considered a divine bond sustaining life.

Thought - provoking prompt
Esoteric Meaning - VERSE 12

In esoteric thought, beauty is often considered a manifestation of the divine. A striking chin, like Lalita Devi's, can be seen as an outward reflection of an inner spiritual radiance. Individuals with heightened spiritual energy often exhibit a luminous complexion.

The Mangalya Sutra, a sacred necklace worn by married Hindu women, holds deeper significance. In yoga, it is likened to the 'bandha', an energetic lock that preserves vital energy within the body. This necklace symbolizes both spiritual grounding and the cyclical nature of life, mirroring the rhythm of breath: inhalation and exhalation.

VERSE 13 - Names 31 and 32

> **Kanak'āngada-keyūra-kamanīya-bhuj'ānvitā,**
> **Ratna-graiveya-chintāka-lola-muktā-phal'ānvitā.**
>
> **Glory! Around Your lovely arms are various bangles and ornaments made of gold; And gem-encrusted pendants and pearl necklaces encircle Your neck.**

Kanak'āngada-keyūra-kamanīya-bhuj'ānvitā - The one who is having bangles and ornaments of gold around beautiful arms
Kanaka - Gold; Āngada - Armlet; Keyūra - Upper Arm Bracelet; Kamanīya - Beautiful; Bhuja - Arm; Ānvitā - Possessing

Ratna-graiveya-chintāka-lola-muktā-phal'ānvitā - The one with gem-encrusted pendants and pearl necklaces encircling the neck
Ratna - Jewel; Graiveya - Necklace; Chintāka - The thinking mind, Tensed Mind, Stressed Mind; Lola - Restless; Muktā - Liberated; Phala - Fruit; Ānvitā - Possessing

Adornment and Divinity

Angada and Keyura are arm ornaments, the former worn closer to the elbow and the latter higher up, towards the shoulder. This verse extols the divine beauty of the Goddess, adorned with golden armlets. These golden ornaments, Kanakāngada and Keyura, were once the hallmark of royal elegance. Gold, a symbol of purity and divinity, reflects the unchanging nature of the Supreme Being. Just as gold is impervious to corrosion, the divine spirit remains untouched by worldly impurities.

The arms, symbolizing action and energy, are adorned with gold to signify the performance of actions with divine grace.

> **"Armlets of gold, a sacred energy's trace, Divine spirit's purity, time cannot erase, Jewel on her heart, love's radiant embrace."**

Devotion and Liberation

Graiveya chintāka are devotees burdened by worldly cares, unable to fully embrace the Goddess within. Through her grace, they evolve into Mukta chintas, devotees free from worldly tensions. The Goddess bestows upon her devotees the fruits of their devotion. The jewel worn by the neck touches the heart and the devotees through her grace are freed from stress with divine love.

Thought - provoking prompt
Esoteric Meaning - VERSE 13

Our elders often spoke of the divine potential inherent in human hands. Diligent action, free from procrastination, is believed to attract prosperity. The gold mentioned in the verse symbolizes the precious, divine energy residing within our hands. This energy empowers us to create abundance. We must invoke Divine energy for strength. However, mere invocation of the divine without corresponding action is insufficient. A harmonious blend of spiritual devotion and practical effort is essential for overcoming life's challenges. By aligning our actions with divine guidance and self-love and love for others, we can transcend stress and attract abundance.

VERSE 14 - Names 33 and 34

> **Kāmeśhwara-prema-ratna-maṇī-prati-paṇa-stanī,
> Nābhy-ālavāla-romāli-latā-phala-kucha-dvayī.**
>
> **Glory! Your bosoms are an expression of the precious
> jewel of the love of Śhrī Śhiva; And hang like fruits on the
> creeper-like line of hair rising from Your navel.**

Kāmeśhwara-prema-ratna-maṇī-prati-paṇa-stanī - The one
whose bosoms are an expression of the precious jewel of the
love of Sri Shiva
Kāmeśhwara - Lord Shiva; Prema - Love; Ratna - Jewel; Maṇī -Gem;
Prati-paṇa - Expressing/Reciprocate; Stanī - Breasts

Nābhy-ālavāla-romāli-latā-phala-kucha-dvayī - The one
whose bosoms hang like fruits on the creeper-like line of hair
rising from the navel.
Nābhya - Navel; Ālavāla - Basin of water around the roots of the tree;
Romāli - A line of body hair above the navel in women; Latā-Creeper;
Phala - Fruit; kucha-dvayī - Both bosoms; Ānvitā -Possessing

A Promise Fulfilled and Divine Motherhood

The verse promises devotees a bountiful return on their devotion:
double the measure of love they offer will be bestowed upon
them. Ultimately, the verse embodies the nurturing aspect of the
divine, comparing the goddess to a mother who sustains and
nourishes her children.

Cosmic Symbolism

The goddess's physical form is imbued with spiritual meaning.
Her bossoms, represented by the creeper from her navel,
symbolize the motherhood, nourishmnet and culmination of
spiritual growth. The delicate hair, resembling a vine, signifies
earthly passions.

The Path to Transcendence

The upward journey of the hair from the lower body represents the spiritual path. It suggests transforming base desires into higher spiritual energies through meditation and devotion.

**Thought - provoking prompt
Esoteric Meaning - VERSE 14**

In esoteric traditions, the number two signifies duality, balance, and the union of the opposites. Thus, double blessings could represent a holistic, transformative grace. The navel is often seen as the cosmic connection point, linking the microcosm (human) to the macrocosm (universe). The creeper emerging from it symbolizes the growth of consciousness from this foundational point. Hair, in many esoteric systems, is associated with vitality, life force, and primal energy. Its upward growth represents the sublimation of these raw energies into higher spiritual states. Breasts, symbolizing motherhood and nourishment, suggest that devotion to the divine is rewarded with abundant blessings, a doubling of what is given and also it represents sustenance, reveals the divine's twofold blessing of abundance and maternal care.

VERSE 15 - Names 35 and 36

> **Lakṣhya-roma-latā-dhāratā-samunneya-madhyamā,**
> **Stana-bhāra-dalan-madhya-paṭṭa-bandha-vali-trayā.**
>
> **Glory! Your waist is so slender it can be adjudged only**
> **from the line of hair; And the three folds on Your stomach**
> **form a support for the weight of Your bosoms.**

Lakṣhya-roma-latā-dhāratā-samunneya-madhyamā - The one whose waist is so slender that it can be adjudged only from the line of hair
Lakṣhya - Distinguishable by; Roma-latā - Line of hair above the navel; Dhāratā - Bearing; Samunneya - Inferred; Madhyamā -Middle waist

Stana-bhāra-dalan-madhya-paṭṭa-bandha-vali-trayā - The one whose three folds on the stomach form a support for the weight of bosoms
Stana bhāra - Weight of breasts; Dalan - Split; Madhya - Mid; Paṭṭa - Crown, Belt; Bandha - Knot; Vali - Fold of skin, Wrinkle; Trayā - Three

The Goddess Graceful Form

The goddess Lalita Devi is described as having a slender, graceful waist, the foundation from which her divine form ascends. This physical perfection symbolizes a deeper spiritual truth: the absence of negative qualities like greed, jealousy, ego, and hatred. A pure and tranquil mind is likened to a flat belly, free from insatiable desires. When these negative impressions are eliminated, one experiences a profound connection with the divine.

The Symbolism of the Waist

Lalita Devi's waist is adorned with three natural lines, resembling a golden belt, which correspond to the three primary energy centers or 'granthis' (Brahma, Vishnu and Rudra Granthis). These lines are also mirrored in the Sri Yantra, a sacred geometric symbol representing the goddess. They signify the three states of consciousness (waking, dreaming, and deep sleep), the three planes of existence (earth, atmosphere, and heavens). In essence, the goddess's form encapsulates the entire cosmos within herself. This description of Lalita Devi suggests that the entire cosmos is contained within her form.

Thought - provoking prompt
Esoteric Meaning - VERSE 15

The description of Lalita Devi provides a rich tapestry of esoteric symbolism. Our form is not merely a physical description but a blueprint of the cosmos, a microcosm reflecting the macrocosm. The focus on inner purity and balance, represented by the slender waist and flat belly, emphasizes the importance of spiritual purification - the absence of negative qualities like greed, jealousy, ego, and hatred as a precursor to spiritual realization.

Ultimately, the esoteric interpretation suggests that by understanding and contemplating the symbolism of Lalita Devi's form, one can gain profound insights into the nature of reality and one's place within it.

VERSE 16 - Names 37 and 38

> Aruṇ'āruṇa-kausumbha-vastra-bhāswat-kaṭī-taṭī,
> Ratna-kinkiṇikā-ramya-raśhanā-dāma-bhūṣhitā.
>
> Glory! Your waist and hips are resplendent in a sari as red
> as the sun; With a golden belt decorated with tiny bells.

Aruṇ'āruṇa-kausumbha-vastra-bhāswat-kaṭī-taṭī - The one
whose waist and hips are resplendent in a sari as red as the
sun.
Āruṇa - Redness; Āruṇa - Redness; Kausumbha - Orange Safflower;
Vastra - Cloth; Bhāswat - Shining; Kaṭī-taṭī - Hips

Ratna-kinkiṇikā-ramya-raśhanā-dāma-bhūṣhitā - The one
whose golden belt is decorated with tiny bells.
Ratna - Jewel; Kinkiṇikā - Small bells; Ramya - Beautiful; Raśhanā -
Belt, Girdle; Dāma - Garland; Bhūṣhitā - Adorned

The Waist Cloth: A Cosmic Tapestry

Lalita Devi's waist cloth is more than mere adornment; it is a
symbolic representation of the cosmos. The fiery red hue,
derived from safflower, echoes the crimson brilliance of celestial
birth. This color also corresponds to the mooladhara chakra, the
foundational energy center associated with creation. The golden
border of the cloth symbolizes the divine energy that envelops
the universe.

The Girdle: A Path to Spiritual Mastery

The gem-studded girdle, raśanādāma, is a microcosm of spiritual
practice. Its name holds a hidden mantra, where each sound
represents an aspect of spiritual discipline: the fire of devotion,
mental control, detachment, sensory restraint, and transcendence
of illusion. By wearing this girdle, Lalita Devi signifies the path
to spiritual mastery through discipline and focus. The girdle's

golden hue mirrors the celestial bodies at the universe's edge, further emphasizing the cosmic connection.

Thought - provoking prompt
Esoteric Meaning - VERSE 16

The fiery red garment reflects the root and sacral chakra, the foundational energy center at the lower waist. Here, creation ignites - the evolution of energy itself. Like gold symbolizing the divine, the garment's golden border represents the divine energy embracing the entire universe.

The waistband further reinforces this concept. It mirrors the celestial bodies at the universe's edge, hinting that the cosmos itself rests within the womb of the cosmic mother. This imagery underscores a profound truth: all creation in this universe stems from the same source, a single, unified energy. This energy not only sparks creation but also sustains it, enveloping all existence in its embrace. It depicts that we all are originated from one source and each of us are the part of that matrix. Everthing in this univese is energy.

VERSE 17 - Names 39 and 40

> **Kāmeśha gñyāta saubhāgya mārdav'oru dvay'ānvitā,**
> **Māṇikya mukuṭ'ākāra jānu dvaya virājitā.**
>
> **Glory! The beauty and smoothness of Your thighs is known only to Lord Śhiva; And Your two knees are like crowns of precious jewels.**

Kāmeśha gñyāta saubhāgya mārdav'oru dvay'ānvitā - The one who possess thighs, the beauty and smoothness of which is known only to Lord Śhiva
Kāmeśha - Shiva; Gñyāta - Known; Saubhāgya - Beauty; Mārdava - Gentleness; Oru - Thigh; Dvaya - Pair; Ānvitā - Having

Māṇikya mukuṭ'ākāra jānu dvaya virājitā - The one who is glorious with knees like two crowns of precious jewels
Māṇiky - Ruby; Mukuṭa - Crown; Ākāra - Shape; Jānu - Knees; Dvaya - Pair; Virājitā - Acclaimed, Exist beautifully

Divine Beauty and Cosmic Womb

The verse extols the sublime beauty of Lalita Devi's lower body, a sacred space likened to the cosmic womb. It suggests that a deep spiritual understanding is essential to appreciate this divine essence, which is beyond the grasp of ordinary consciousness.

The Human Body: A Vessel for Potential

The imagery of Lalita Devi's knees as jeweled crowns symbolizes human potential. Just as strong knees are crucial for physical mobility, determination and perseverance are essential for navigating life's journey. This verse implies that the human body is a perfect instrument for achieving one's goals when coupled with focused effort.

Thought - provoking prompt
Esoteric Meaning - VERSE 17

The text alludes to profound esoteric concepts, suggesting that the physical body is a microcosm of the cosmos. The divine feminine, represented by Lalita Devi, is the creative force underlying all existence. To truly understand one's nature and purpose, a spiritual journey is necessary, one that involves activating the inner potential through disciplines like yoga and meditation. The comparison of the knees to jeweled crowns is more than a poetic device. In esoteric traditions, the human body is seen as a microcosm of the universe. The knees, as the foundation for movement, represent grounding and stability. The verse suggests that through concentrated effort and unwavering commitment, the human body can be transformed into a vessel capable of extraordinary feats.

VERSE 18 - Names 41 to 43

> **Indra-gopa-pari-kṣhipta-smara-tūṇābha-jaṅghikā,**
> **Gūḍha-gulphā,Kūrma-pṛiṣhtha-jayiṣhṇu-prapad'ānvitā.**
>
> **Glory! Your calves are the quivers of the God of Love covered with sparkling jewels; With hidden ankles, and the fore-feet shaped like tortoise-shells.**

Indra-gopa-pari-kṣhipta-smara-tūṇābha-jaṅghikā - The one whose gleaming calves are the quivers of the God of Love covered with fire-flies
Indra-gopa - fire fly (protected by Indra); Pari-kṣhipta - Covered; Smara - Resembling; Tūṇa - Holder, Quiver; Ābha - Shining; Janghika - Calves

Gūḍha-gulphā - The one with hidden ankles
Gūḍha - Hidden; Gulphā - Ankle

Kūrma-pṛiṣhtha-jayiṣhṇu-prapad'ānvitā - The one whose feet are shaped like the back of tortoise-shells
Kūrma - Tortoise; Pṛiṣhtha - The back (the shell); Jayiṣhṇu -Victorious; Prapada - Front of foot; Ānvitā - Furnished with,Graced

Calves as Symbols of Passionate Power

The verse extols the beauty and symmetry of Lalita Devi's calves, comparing them to Cupid's quiver. It suggests that her calves possess a magnetic power capable of igniting passion even in the heart of the passionless Shiva. This imagery implies that strong calves are a symbol of vital energy, which contributes to overall health and vitality, allowing one to live life to the fullest.

Feet as Embodiments of Divine Strength and Grace

Lalita Devi's feet are described with reverence, compared to the back of a tortoise – a symbol of steadfastness and strength. This comparison highlights the firmness, softness, and beauty of her feet. The legend of the tortoise supporting Mount Meru during the churning of the ocean adds a divine dimension to the imagery, suggesting that her feet are a foundation of strength and grace, capable of supporting great endeavors and yielding auspicious results.

Thought - provoking prompt
Esoteric Meaning - VERSE 18

Legs are the instruments through which we physically interact with the world. They carry us forward, allowing us to explore, conquer, and create. In the context of the verse, Lalita Devi's calves, equated with Cupid's quiver, suggest very being is a force of action, capable of inspiring and motivating others. Legs provide the support and power necessary for movement. Strong legs are often associated with vitality, courage, and determination. By describing Lalita Devi's calves as strong, the verses emphasizes inner power and resilience. Legs connect us to the earth, providing a sense of stability and balance. The comparison of Lalita Devi's feet to the tortoise, a symbol of grounding, reinforces this idea.

VERSE 19 - Names 44 and 45

> **Nakha-dīdhiti-sam-chhanna-namaj-jana-tamo-guṇā,
> Pada-dvaya-prabhā-jāla-parākrita-saroruhā.**
>
> **Glory! The brilliance of Your toenails dispels the darkness
> of Tamo Guna of those who bow to You; And Your Holy Feet
> defeat the Lotus in radiant beauty.**

Nakha-dīdhiti-sam-chhanna-namaj-jana-tamo-guṇā - The Brilliance of whose toenails dispels the darkness of Tamo Guna of those who bow to You
Nakha - Nails; Dīdhiti - Bright; Sam-chhanna - Entirely covered; Namaj - Bowing; Jana - Creatures; Tamo - Ignorance; Guṇā - Quality

Pada-dvaya-prabhā-jāla-parākrita-saroruhā - The one whose two holy feet defeat the Lotus in radiant beauty
Pada - Feet; Dvyaya - Pair, Two; Prabhā - Radiance; Jāla - Illusion, Trap; Parākrita - Set aside; Saroruhā - Lotus

Dispelling Ignornace and Blessing with Feet

The radiant light emanating from fingernails is said to dispel the "tamo guna" (darkness, inertia) and ignorance of devotees. This suggests that her mere presence of divine energy illuminates the path for those who seek blessings. The text explains that four hands (functional nature) are occupied with weapons, signifying power and ability to protect. Since they cannot be used for blessings, feet assume this role. The ten nails of Lalita Devi are likened to the ten principal Upanishads, ancient scriptures containing profound wisdom. This connection suggests that her blessings impart the knowledge to dispel ignorance, residing within our own consciousness.

> **"Light from her toes, a knowledge bestowed, Heart-
> lotus fragrant, where her grace has flowed."**

Feet and Ever-presence Grace

The text beautifully compares Lalita Devi's feet to lotuses, surpassing them in radiance, softness, purity, and fragrance. This emphasizes the divine quality of her feet. The final lines highlight the presence of Lalita Devi's glowing feet in the devotee's heart lotus. This signifies a deep devotional connection, where the divine resides within the devotee.

**Thought - provoking prompt
Esoteric Meaning - VERSE 19**

Building upon the preceding verse's emphasis on action and grounding, this stanza delves into the inner dimension of spiritual growth. It posits that all scriptural wisdom is inherent within our consciousness, accessible through a calm and receptive state of mind. Lalita Devi's feet, symbolizing a profound connection to the divine, provide a steadfast foundation for individuals to embark on this inward journey. By rooting oneself in this divine wisdom, one can dispel negativity, darkness, inertia and undertake actions with greater clarity, purpose, and likelihood of positive outcomes.

VERSE 20 - Names 46 to 48

> Siñjāna-maṇi-mañjīra-maṇḍita-śhrī-pad'āmbujā,
> Marālī-manda-gamanā-Mahā-lāvaṇya-śhevadhiḥ.
>
> Glory! Your Sacred Lotus-Feet are adorned with jingling
> anklets; And Your gait is graceful like a swan, O Great
> Treasure-house of Beauty.

Siñjāna-maṇi-mañjīra-maṇḍita-śhrī-pad'āmbujā - The One whose sacred Lotus-Feet are adorned with jingling anklets
Siñjāna - tinkling, jingling; Maṇi - beads; Mañjīra - anklet; Maṇḍita - adorned; Śhrī-pad - Sacred feet; Āmbujā - Like the lotus (ambu-water, ja-born)

Marālī-manda-gamanā - The one whose languid gait is graceful like a swan
Marālī - Swan; Manda - Slow moving; Gamanā - Gait, style of walk

Mahā-lāvaṇya-śhevadhiḥ - The Treasure-house of Great Beauty
Mahā - Great; Lāvaṇya - Beautiful; śhevadhiḥ - Treasure house

The Music of Action

Lalita Devi's anklets, adorned with precious gems, emit a melodious chime. This musicality symbolizes the fruitful outcome of actions performed with divine intent. The verse implies that by aligning actions with spiritual purpose, one can harvest bountiful rewards. Lotus is linked with auspiciousness and abundance.

The Art of Divine Pace

Likened to a graceful swan, Lalita Devi's gait embodies the perfect balance between haste and delay. This serves as a spiritual guide, emphasizing the importance of steady, consistent effort without rushing or procrastinating. The verse suggests that finding this equilibrium is essential for spiritual growth and fulfillment.

Thought - provoking prompt
Esoteric Meaning - VERSE 20

The anklets of Lalita Devi can be interpreted esoterically as representing the subtle vibrations or cosmic harmonics that underlie creation. The "melodious sounds" they produce might symbolize the music of the spheres, a concept found in many ancient philosophies, representing the underlying order of the universe. The idea that these sounds are the fruits of actions suggests that our actions, when aligned with cosmic rhythms, create harmonious outcomes. The swan, in many spiritual traditions, symbolizes purity and divine consciousness. Its slow, graceful movement can be seen as a metaphor for the spiritual as well as any journey of life. The instruction to move neither too fast nor too slow implies the importance of balance and mindfulness in any practice. It suggests that the path to enlightenment or any work is not about rushing or delaying but about a steady, conscious progression.

VERSE 21 - Names 49 to 54

> Sarv'āruṇā, Anavady'āṇgī, Sarv'ābharaṇa-bhūṣhitā,
> Śhiva-kāmeśhwar'āṇkasthā, Śhivā-Swādhīna-vallabhā.
>
> Glory! Wholly rosy, Your body is faultlessly beautiful,
> adorned with every ornament; Seated on the thigh of Lord
> Śhiva, You are His Other Half, and He is completely Your
> own.

Sarv'āruṇā - The one who is Wholly rosy
Sarva - Everything, All; Āruṇā - Red

Anavady'āṇgī - The one whose body is faultlessly beautiful
Anavadya - Faultless; Āṇgī - Body, Limbs

Sarv'ābharaṇa-bhūṣhitā - The one who is adorned with every ornament
Sarva - All, Everything; Ābharaṇa - Ornaments; Bhūṣhitā - Adorned

Śhiva-kāmeśhwar'āṇkasthā - The one who is seated on the thigh of Śhrī Śhiva
Śhiva - Kāmeśhwara - The auspicious Lord Shiva; Āṇka - Thigh; Sthā - Stationed

Śhivā - The one who is the other half of Śhrī Śhiva
Śhivā - Lord Shiva

Swādhīna-vallabhā - The one who has completely won over her beloved
Swādhīna - Independent, Free - willed; Vallabhā - Beloved

Lalita Devi: The Divine Feminine Embodied

The verse paints a resplendent image of Lalita Devi, describing
her as a flawless embodiment of divine beauty. Her form is
depicted as a harmonious blend of the formless (Nirguna
Brahman) and the manifest (Saguna Brahman). Adorned with the

cosmos as her ornaments, she is a living representation of the universe. This verse suggests that meditating on her cosmic form can lead to abundance and fulfillment.

The Cosmic Dance of Shiva and Shakti

The concept of Lalita Devi seated on Shiva's lap symbolizes the interplay of the static and dynamic principles of creation. Shiva represents the unchanging consciousness, while Shakti is the dynamic cosmic energy responsible for creation, preservation, and destruction. This dynamic interplay is further exemplified by the image of Kali dancing on Shiva. The verse underscores the inseparable nature of the divine masculine and feminine, emphasizing Shakti's dominance and control over the cosmic forces.

In essence, this passage delves into the profound philosophical and cosmological dimensions of Lalita Devi, positioning her as both the supreme being and the animating force of the universe.

Thought - provoking prompt
Esoteric Meaning - VERSE 21

The initial verses of the Lalita Sahasranama establish a profound connection between the human body and the cosmos. By meticulously describing the physical form, the text invites contemplation on the intricate harmony and complexity of existence. This microcosmic perspective expands outward, suggesting that the human body is a miniature replica of the universe, adorned with celestial lights.

The introduction of Shiva and Shakti into this cosmic framework reveals the divine undercurrent of human existence. The concept of "I am Shiva" (SHIVOHAM) places the individual at the center of the divine experience. This self-realization, coupled with the dynamic energy of Shakti, forms the creative force within each person.

Ultimately, the passage culminates in the recognition of ourselves as the embodiment of the unified Shiva and Shakti. This divine union, expressed through playful interaction, is seen as the fundamental principle animating the universe.

In essence, these verses offer a holistic worldview, inviting readers to explore the divine within, recognizing the human body as a sacred temple, and the universe as an extension of the self.

VERSE 22 - Names 55 to 58

> Sumeru-madhya-sṛiṅgha-sthā,Shrīman-nagara-nāyikā,
> Chintāmaṇi-gṛihānta-sthā,Pañcha-brahm'āsana-sthitā.
>
> Glory! Residing on the middle peak of Mount Meru, You are Queen of the Auspicious City; Occupying the mansion of wish-fulfilling gems,on a couch of the five aspects of God.

Sumeru-madhya-sṛiṅgha-sthā - The one who is standing on the middle peak of Mount Meru
Sumeru - Mount Meru; Madhya - Middle; Sṛiṅgha - Peak; Sthā - Residing

Shrīman-nagara-nāyikā - The one who is the Queen of the Auspicious City
Shrīman - Royal; Nagara - Town; Nāyikā - Leader, Heroine

Chintāmaṇi-gṛihānta-sthā - The one who is residing in the mansion of wish-fulfilling gems
Chintāmaṇi - Wish Fulfilling Gem; Gṛihā - House; Ānta-Sthā -Staying At The End

Pañcha-brahm'āsana-sthitā - The one who is seated on a throne of the five aspects of God
Pañcha - Five; Brahma - Formless God; Āsana - Seated; Sthitā -Sitting

The Human Body as a Sacred Geometry

This verse unveils the esoteric connection between the human body and the cosmic blueprint known as the Sri Yantra. It posits that the body is a microcosmic representation of this sacred geometric form, with the crown chakra serving as the central point of divine energy.

> "Sri Yantra within, the body's sacred art, Lalita's bindu, where divine wishes start."

Lalita Devi: The Indwelling Goddess

The verse places Lalita Devi at the heart of both the Sri Yantra and the human body. She is described as the eternal presence within the central bindu, the source of all creation. This suggests that the divine feminine principle is inherent in every individual. This temple - our human body and our consciouness helps us in fulfilling all our wishes.

The Divine Throne

The image of Lalita Devi seated on a throne supported by the five elements (Earth, Water, Fire, Air, Space) establishes her as the supreme cosmic ruler. This reinforces the idea that the goddess is the underlying force governing the universe and human existence.

Thought - provoking prompt
Esoteric Meaning - VERSE 22

The verse unveils the human body as a microcosmic representation of the divine cosmic blueprint, the Sri Yantra. Lalita Devi, the divine feminine principle, is identified as the indwelling consciousness within this sacred geometry. Her presence signifies the potential for divine realization inherent in every individual and also the wish fulfilling potential. The verse ultimately suggests that through understanding and contemplating one's own body as a sacred space, one can access the divine within.

VERSE 23 - Names 59 to 63

> Mahā-padmātavi-samsthā,Kadamba-vana-vāsinī ,
> Sudhā-sāgara-madhya-sthā,Kām'ākṣhī-kāma-dāyinī.
>
> Glory! You dwell in the great Lotus forest, residing in the
> forest of kadamba trees, Standing in the middle of the
> ocean of nectar, You are the lovely-eyed, fulfiller of all

Mahā-padm'āṭavi sam-sthā - The one who is dwelling in the great Lotus forest

Mahā-Great; Padma-Lotus; Āṭavi-Forest; Sam-Sthā-Residing

Kadamba-vana-vāsinī - The one who is residing in the forest of wish-fulfilling and grace showering trees

Kadamba- Grace showering and Wish Fulilling Tree; Vana-Forest; Vāsinī- Dwelling

Sudhā-sāgara-madhya-sthā - The one who is standing in the the ocean of nectar

Sudhā- Nectar, Divine Ambrosia; Sāgara- Ocean; madhya-sthā- Middle Staying

Kām'ākṣhī - The one who is Lovely-eyed

Kāma- Lovely; Ākṣhī- Eyes

Kāma-dāyinī - The one who is the fulfiller of all desires

Kāma- Love, Desire; Dāyinī- Grantor

The Universe as a Lotus Garden

This verse presents a cosmic perspective, likening the universe to a vast garden of lotus flowers. The lotus, a symbol of spiritual awakening, represents the potential for consciousness to unfold within all beings. The lotus is a symbol of purity and divine creation. A lotus forest signifies a spiritual realm of supreme beauty and purity. The term "Mahā padmāṭavī" suggests that the universe is a field of consciousness waiting to be illuminated.

Lalita Devi as Cosmic Energy

Lalita Devi is identified with the cosmic energy that animates this lotus garden. As Kundalini Shakti, she resides within the subtle energy centers (chakras) of the human body, mirroring the cosmic structure. The concept of "Kadamba vana vāsinī" introduces the idea of the universe as a product of the divine union of Shiva (consciousness) and Shakti (energy) and its capability of fulfilling our desires. The Kadamba tree is often associated with love and devotion. This also represents Heart Chakra. Residing in such a grove implies a place of intense love and devotion.

The Oceanic Depths of Consciousness

The image of Lalita Devi as "Sudhā-sāgara-madhya-sthā" places her at the heart of the oceanic depths of consciousness. The Sahasrara chakra, often associated with this "ocean of nectar," is the locus of divine union. The names "Kāmākṣī" and "Kāmadāyinī" emphasize the creative and sustaining aspects of this divine energy. Kāmākṣī has many meanings. The most ordinary meaning is a beautiful lady whose eyes are full of passion. Among our five senses, eyes are of foremost importance. Kāmadāyinī means one who grants various boons to fulfill our desires. It could also mean 'one who grants kama or passion' i.e. the energy needed for our sustenance.

Thought - provoking prompt
Esoteric Meaning - VERSE 23

The verse offers a view of existence as a vast, interconnected realm of potential, depicted as a lotus garden awaiting the activation of divine consciousness. This consciousness, embodied by Lalita Devi as Kundalini Shakti, serves as the vital energy animating both the universe and the individual's subtle energy centers. The image of an "ocean of nectar" further symbolizes the profound depths of consciousness, a primordial, undifferentiated state from which all creation emerges. Lalita Devi, at the heart of this ocean, represents the divine source, responsive to love and devotion, and always ready to fulfill the wishes of those who approach her with affection. Ultimately, the verse proposes a non-dualistic understanding, where the individual is a reflection of the cosmic whole, immersed in the same oceanic consciousness. Spiritual practice is presented as the means to awaken this inner potential and realize one's inherent divinity.

Chapter 7: Lalita Sahasranama Stotram: The Complete Hymn

This chapter presents the complete Lalita Sahasranama for chanting, aiming to unlock its profound wisdom and power.

In Hinduism, the Lalita Sahasranama is a revered hymn enshrined within the Brahmanda Purana. It unfolds the multifaceted essence of the goddess Lalita Devi, also known as Tripura Sundari, through 1000 poetic names/183 poetic verses. Each name, like a brushstroke, paints a unique aspect, quality, or characteristic of the divine.

ŚHRĪ LALITĀ SAHASRA-NĀMA STOTRAM
The Thousand Names of Śhrī Lalitā
as a poem

Om Śhrī Gaṇeśhāya namaḥ

'Salutations to the Lord of Ganas and Remover of Obstacles'

Dedication:

Asyā-Śhrī-Lalitā-sahasra-nāma-stotra-mālā-mahā-mantrasya.

Of this garland of mighty mantras of the Thousand Names of Śhrī Lalitā.

Vaśhiny-ādi-vāg-devatā-ṛiṣhayaḥ.

The Composing Seers are Vāśhini and the other Vāg-devatās.

Anuṣhṭup-chhandaḥ.

The metre is Anuṣtubh.

Śhrī-Lalitā-parameśhvarī-devatā.

The Presiding Deity is the Supreme Goddess Śhrī Lalitā.

Aiṁ-bījam,Sauḥ-śhaktiḥ,Klīṁ-kilakam.

Aim is the seed, Sauḥ is the power, Klīm is the door-latch.

Śhrī-Lalitā-mahā-tripura-sundarī-cintitaphalāvāptyarthe-prasād-siddhy-artha-jape viniyogaḥ.

This recitation is undertaken to obtain the desired result of a thought and to please Śhrī Lalitā Mahā-Tripura-Sundarī.

(Impotant Note: Breathe in, hold the breath and then ask for wish and then breathe out)

MEDITATION:

> Sindūr'āruṇa-vigrahām-tri-nayanām
> Māṇikya-mauli-sphurat-tārā-nāyaka-śhekharām
> Smita-mukhim-āpīna-vakṣhoruhām.
> Pāṇim-yāmali-pūrṇa-ratna-chaṣhakam
> Rakt'otpalam-bibhratīm-saumyām-ratna-ghaṭa-stha
> Rakta-charaṇām-dhyāyet-par'āmbikām..

I meditate upon the Supreme Mother, red like Sindūr powder, three-eyed, with the crescent Moon as her crest jewel, who is adorned a crown of gems, with an enchanting smiling indicating compassion and have well-formed bosoms. In Her hands she bears a red Lotus, and a precious cup of Nectar. She is cheerful and her red feet rest on a water-pot encrusted with precious stones.

> aruṇām-karuṇā-taraṅgitākṣīm
> dhṛta pāśāṅkuśa puṣpa bāṇacāpām.
> aṇimādibhi rāvṛtām mayūkhai-
> rahamityeva vibhāvaye bhavānīm..

I meditate upon the Great Empress. She is red in color, and her eyes are full of compassion, and holds the noose, the goad, the bow and the flowery arrows in her hands. She is sorrounded on all sides by powers such as Anima for rays and she is the self within me.

> dhyāyet-padmāsanasthām-vikasitavadanā-
> padmapatrāyatākṣīm
> hemābhām-pītavastrām-karakalitalasaddhemapadmām-
> varāṅgīm.
> sarvālaṅkāra-yuktām-satata-mabhayadām-bhaktanamrām
> bhavānīm
> śrīvidyām-śānta-mūrtim-sakala-suranutām-sarva-
> sampatpradātrīm..

I meditate upon the Divine Goddess who is seated on the lotus with petal eyes. She is golden hued, and has a lotus flowers in her hand. She dispels fear of the devotees who bow before her. She is the embodiment of peace, knowledge, is praised by gods and grants every kind of wealth wished for.

> sakuṅkuma-vilepanāmalikacumbi-kastūrikāṃ
> samanda-hasitekṣaṇāṃ-saśara-cāpa-pāśāṅkuśām.
> aśeṣajana-mohinīṃ-aruṇa-mālya-bhūṣāmbarāṃ
> japākusuma-bhāsurāṃ-japavidhau-smare-dambikām..

I meditate upon the Mother, whose eyes are smiling, who holds the arrow, bow, noose and goad in her hands. She is glittering with red garlands and ornaments. She is painted with Kumkum on her forehead and is red and tender like the Japa flower.

Śhrī-mātā,Śhrī-mahā-rājñī,Śhrī-mat-simh'āsan'eśhvarī,
Chid-agni-kuṇḍa-sambhūtā,Deva-kārya-samudyatā. (1)

Udyad-bhānu-sahasrābhā,Chatur-bāhu-samanvitā,
Rāga-swarūpa-paśh'āḍhyā,Krodh'ākār'ānkuśh'ojjvalā. (2)

Mano-rūp'ekṣhu-kodaṇḍā,Pañcha-tanmātra-sāyakā,
Nij'āruṇa-prabhā-pūra-majjad-brahmāṇḍa-maṇḍalā. (3)

Champak'āśhoka-punnāga-saugandhika-lasat-kachā,
Kuruvinda-maṇi-śhreṇī-kanat-koṭīra-maṇḍitā. (4)

Aṣhṭamī-chandra-vibhrāja-dalika-sthala-śhobhitā,
Mukha-chandra-kalaṅkābha-mṛiga-nābhi-viśheṣhakā. (5)

Vadana-smara-māṅgalya-gṛiha-toraṇa-chillikā,
Vaktra-lakshmi-parīvāha-chalan-mīn'ābha-lochanā. (6)

Nava-champaka-puṣhpābha-nāsā-ḍaṇḍa-virājitā,
Tārā-kānti-tiras-kāri-nāsā-bharaṇa-bhāsurā. (7)

Kadamba-mañjari-klṛipta-karṇa-pūra-manoharā,
Tāṭanka-yugalī-bhūta-tapan-oḍupa-maṇḍalā. (8)

Padma-rāga-śhil'ādarśha-pari-bhāvi-kapola-bhūḥ,
Nava-vidruma-bimba-śhrī-nyak-kāri-radanach-chhadā. (9)

Śhuddha-vidy'āṅkur-ākāra-dvija-pankti-dvay'ojjvalā,
Karpūra-vītikā-moda-samākarṣhi-digantarā. (10)

Nija-sallāpa-mādhurya-vinir-bhartsita-kachchhapī,
Manda-smita-prabhāpūra-majjat-kāmeśha-mānasā. (11)

Anākalita-sādṛiśhya-chibuka-śhrī-virājitā,
Kāmeśha-baddha-māṅgalya-sūtra-śhobhita-kandharā. (12)

Kanak'āngada-keyūra-kamanīya-bhujānvitā,
Ratna-graiveya-chintāka-lola-muktā-phal'ānvitā. (13)

Kāmeśhwara-prema-ratna-maṇī-prati-paṇa-stanī,
Nābhy-ālavāla-romāli-latā-phala-kucha-dvayī. (14)

Lakṣhya-roma-latādhāra-ta-samunneya-madhyamā,
Stana-bhāra-dalan-madhya-paṭṭa-bandha-vali-trayā.(15)

Aruṇ'āruṇa-kausumbha-vastra-bhāswat-kaṭī-taṭī,
Ratna-kinkiṇikā-ramya-raśhanā-dāma-bhūṣhitā. (16)

Kāmeśha-gñyāta-saubhāgya-mārda-voru-dvay'ānvitā,
Māṇikya-mukuṭ'ākāra-jānu-dvaya-virājitā. (17)

Indra-gopa-parikṣhipta-smara-tūṇābha-jaṅghikā,
Gūḍha-gulphā-kūrma-pṛiṣhtha-jayiṣhṇu-prapad'ānvitā. (18)

Nakha-dīdhiti-samchhanna-namaj-jana-tamo-guṇā ,
Pada-dvaya-prabhājāla-parākṛita-saroruhā. (19)

Siñjāna-maṇi-mañjīra-maṇḍita-Śhrī-pad'āmbujā,
Marālī-manda-gamanā,Mahā-lāvaṇya-śhevadhiḥ. (20)

Sarv'āruṇ'ānavady'āṅgī,Sarv'ābharaṇa-bhūṣhitā,
Śhiva-kāmeśhwar'āṅkasthā,Śhivā-Swādhīna-vallabhā. (21)

Sumeru-madhya-sṛiṅgha-sthā,Śhrīman-nagara-nāyikā,
Chintāmaṇi-gṛihānta-sthā,Pañcha-brahm'āsana-sthitā. (22)

Mahā-padmāṭavi-samsthā,Kadamba-vana-vāsinī ,
Sudhā-sāgara-madhya-sthā,Kām'ākṣhī-kāma-dāyinī. (23)

Devarṣhi-gaṇa-saṅghāta-stūya-mān'ātma-vaibhavā,
Bhaṇḍāsura-vadh'odyukta-śhakti-senā-sam-anvitā. (24)

Sampat-karī-sam-ārūḍha-sindhura-vraja-sevitā ,
Aśhwārūḍh'ādhi-ṣhṭhit'āswa-koṭi-koṭibhir-āvṛitā. (25)

Chakra-rāja-rath'ārūḍha-sarv'āyudha-pariśh-kṛitā,
Geya-chakra-rath'ārūḍha-mantriṇī-pari-sevitā. (26)

Kiri-chakra-rath'ārūḍha-daṇḍa-nāthā-puraskṛitā,
Jvālā-mālini-kākṣhipta-vahni-prākāra-madhya-gā. (27)

Bhaṇḍa-sainyā-vadh'od-yukta-śhaktī-vikrama-harṣhitā,
Nityā-par'ākram'āṭopa-nirīkṣhaṇa-sam-utsukā. (28)

Bhaṇḍa-putra-vadh'od-yukta-bālā-vikrama-nanditā ,
Mantriṇy'ambā-virachita-viṣhāṅga-vadha-toṣhitā. (29)

Viśhukra-prāṇa-haraṇa-vārāhī-vīrya-nanditā,
Kāmeśhwara-mukhāloka-kalpita-śhrī-gaṇeśhvarā. (30)

Mahā-gaṇeśha-nirbhinna-vighna-yantra-praharṣhitā,
Bhaṇḍ'āsurendra-nirmukta-śhastra-praty'astra-varṣhiṇī (31)

Kar'āṅguli-nakh'otpanna-nārāyaṇa-daśh'ākṛitiḥ,
Mahā-pāśhupat'āstrāgni-nirdagdh'āsura-sainikā. (32)

Kāmeśhvar'āstra-nirdagdha-sa-bhaṇḍāsura-śhūnyakā,
Brahm'opendra-mahendr'ādi-deva-samstuta-vaibhavā. (33)

Hara-netr'āgni-sam-dagdha-kāma-saṅjīvan'auṣhadhiḥ,
Śhrīmad-vāg-bhava-kūtaika-swarūpa-mukha-paṅkajā. (34)

Kaṇṭh'ādhaḥ-kaṭi-paryanta-madhya-kūṭa-swarūpiṇī,
Śhakti-kūṭaika-tāpanna-kaṭyadho-bhāga-dhariṇī. (35)

Mūla-mantr'ātmikā,Mūla-kūṭa-traya-kalebarā,
Kul'āmṛit'aika-rasika,Kula-saṅketa-pālinī. (36)

Kul'āṅganā,kul'ānta-sthā,Kaulinī,Kula-yoginī,
Akula,Samay'ānta-sthā,Samay'āchāra-tatparā. (37)

Mūlādhār'aika-nilayā,Brahma-granthi-vibhedinī,
Maṇipur'āntar-uditā,Viṣhṇu-granthi-vibhedinī. (38)

Agñyā-chakr'āntarala-sthā,Rudra-granthi-vibhedinī,
Sahasrār'āmbuj'ārūḍhā,Sudhā-sār'ābhi-varṣhiṇī. (39)

Taḍillata-sama-ruchiḥ,ṣhat-chakr'opari-samsthitā,
Mahā-śhaktiḥ,Kuṇḍalinī,Bisa-tantu-tanīyasī. (40)

Bhavānī,Bhāvan'āgamyā,Bhav'āraṇya-kuṭhārikā,
Bhadra-priyā,Bhadra-mūrtir,Bhaktā-saubhāgya-dāyinī. (41)

Bhakti-priyā,Bhakti-gamyā,Bhakti-vaśhyā,Bhay'āpahā,
Śhāmbhavī,Śhārad'ārādhyā,Śharvaṇī,Śharma-dāyinī. (42)

Śham-karī,Śhrī-karī,Sādhvī,Śharach-chandra-nibh'ānanā,
Śhāt-odarī,Śhānti-matī,Nir-ādhārā,Nir-añjanā. (43)

Nirlepā,Nirmalā,Nityā,Nir-ākārā,Nir-ākulā ,
Nirguṇā,Niṣhkalā,Śhāntā,Niṣhkāmā,Nir-upaplavā. (44)

Nitya-muktā,Nir-vikarā,Niṣh-prapañchā,Nir-āśhrayā,
Nitya-śhuddhā,Nitya-buddhā,Nir-avadyā,Nir-antarā. (45)

Niṣh-kāraṇā,Niṣh-kalaṅkā,Nir-upādhir,Nir-īśhwarā,
Nīrāgā,Rāga-mathanī,Nirmadā,Mada-nāśhinī. (46)

Nischintā,Nir-ahaṁkarā,Nir-mohā,Moha-nāśhinī,
Nirmamā,Mamatā-hantrī,Niṣhpāpā,Pāpa-nāśhinī. (47)

Niṣh-krodhā,Krodha-śhamanī,Nir-lobhā,Lobha-nāśhinī,
Niḥ-samśhayā,Samśhaya-ghnī,Nir-bhavā,Bhava-nāśhinī. (48)

Nir-vikalpā,Nir-ābādhā,Nirbhedā,Bheda-nāśhinī ,
Nir-nāśhā,Mṛityu-mathanī,Niṣhkriyā,Niṣh-parigrahā. (49)

Nistulā,Nīla-chikurā,Nirapāyā,Niratyayā,
Dur-labhā,Dur-gamā,Durgā,Duḥkha-hantrī,Sukha-pradā. (50)

Dushṭa-dūrā,Dur-āchāra-śhamanī,Doṣha-varjitā,
Sarva-gñyā,Sāndra-karuṇā,Samānādhika-varjitā. (51)

Sarva-śhakti-mayī,Sarva-maṅgalā,Sad-gati-pradā,
Sarveśhwarī,Sarva-mayī,Sarva-mantra-swarūpiṇī. (52)

Sarva-yantr-ātmikā,Sarva-tantra-rūpā,Man'on-manī,
Maheśhwarī,Mahādevī,Mahā-lakṣhmī,Mṛiḍa-priyā. (53)

Mahā-rūpā,Mahā-pūjyā,Mahā-pātaka-nāśhinī,
Mahā-māyā,Mahā-sattwā,Mahā-śhaktir,Mahā-ratiḥ. (54)

Mahā-bhogā,Mah'aiswaryā,Mahā-viryā,Mahā-balā,
Mahā-buddhir,Mahā-siddhir,Mahā-yogeśhwar'eśhwarī. (55)

Mahā-tantrā,Mahā-mantrā,Mahā-yantrā,Mahāsanā,
Mahā-yaga-kram'ārādhyā,Mahā-bhairava-pūjitā. (56)

Maheśhvara-mahā-kalpa-mahā-tāṇḍava-sākṣhiṇī,
Mahā-kāmeśha-mahiṣhī,Mahā-tripura-sundarī. (57)

Chatuḥ-ṣhaṣhṭy'upa-chārādhyā,Chatuḥ-ṣhaṣhṭi-kalā-mayī,
Mahā-chatuḥ-ṣhaṣhti-koṭi-yoginī-gaṇa-sevitā. (58)

Manu-vidyā,Chandra-vidyā,Chandra-maṇḍala-madhya-gā,
Chāru-rūpā,Chāru-hāsā,Chāru-chandra-kalā-dharā. (59)

Char'āchara-jagan-nāthā,Chakra-rāja-niketanā,
Pārvatī,Padma-nayanā,Padma-rāga-sama-prabhā. (60)

Pañcha-pret'āsan-āsīnā, Pañcha-brahma-swarūpiṇī,
Chin-mayī, Param-ānandā, Vigñyāna-ghana-rūpiṇī. (61)

Dhyāna-dhyātṛi-dhyeya-rūpā, Dharm'ādharma-vivarjitā,
Viśhwa-rūpā, Jāgariṇī, Swapantī, Taijas-ātmikā. (62)

Suptā, Prāgñy'ātmikā, Turyā, Sarv'āvasthā-vivarjitā,
Sṛiṣhṭi-kartrī, Brahma-rūpā, Goptrī, Govinda-rūpiṇī. (63)

Saṃhāriṇī, Rudra-rūpā, Tirodhāna-karī, Īśhvarī,
Sadā-śhiva, 'Ānu-graha-dā, Pañcha-kṛitya-parāyaṇā. (64)

Bhānu-maṇḍala-madhya-sthā, Bhairavī, Bhaga-mālinī,
Padmāsanā, Bhagavatī, Padma-nābha-sahodarī. (65)

Unmeṣha-nimiṣh'otpanna-vipanna-bhuvan'āvalī,
Sahasra-śhīrṣha-vadanā, Sahasr'ākṣhī, Sahasra-pāt. (66)

Ā-brahma-kiṭa-jananī, Varṇ'āśhrama-vidhāyinī ,
Nij'āgñyā-rūpa-nigamā, Puṇy'āpuṇya-phala-pradā.(67)

Śhruti-sīmanta-sindūrī-kṛita-pādābja-dhūlikā,
Sakal'āgama-saṃdoha-śhukti-saṃpuṭa-mauktikā. (68)

Puruṣh'ārtha-pradā, Pūrṇā, Bhoginī, Bhuvaneśhvarī,
Ambik'ānādi-nidhanā, Hari-brahm'endra-sevitā. (69)

Nārāyaṇī, nāda-rūpā, Nāma-rūpa-vivarjitā,
Hrīṃ-kārī, Hrīṃ-matī, Hṛidyā, Heyopādeya-varjitā. (70)

Rāja-rāj'ārchitā,Rājñī,Ramyā,Rājīva-lochanā,
Rañjanī,Ramaṇī,Rasyā,Raṇat-kiṅkiṇi-mekhalā. (71)

Ramā,Rākendu-vadanā,Rati-rūpā,Rati-priyā ,
Rakṣhā-karī,Rākṣhasa-ghnī,Rāmā,Ramaṇa-lampaṭā. (72)

Kāmyā,Kāma-kalā-rūpā,Kadamba-kusuma-priyā,
Kalyāṇī,Jagatī-kandā,Karuṇā-rasa-sāgarā. (73)

Kalā-vatī,Kal'ālāpā,Kāntā,Kādambarī-priyā,
Varadā,Vāma-nayanā,Vāruṇī-mada-vihvalā. (74)

Viśhw'ādhikā,Veda-vedyā,Vindhy'āchala-nivāsinī,
Vidhātrī,Veda-jananī,Viṣhṇu-māyā,Vilāsinī. (75)

Kṣhetra-swarūpā,Kṣhetreśhī,Kṣhetra-kṣhetra-gñya-pālinī,
Kṣhaya-vṛiddhi-vinir-muktā,Kṣhetra-pāla-sam-architā. (76)

Vijayā,Vimalā,Vandyā,Vandāru-jana-vatsalā ,
Vāg-vadinī,Vāmakeśhī,Vahni-maṇḍala-vāsinī. (77)

Bhakti-mat-kalpa-latikā,Paśhu-pāśha-vimochinī,
Saṁ-hṛit'āśheṣha-pāṣhaṇḍā,Sad-āchāra-pra-vartikā. (78)

Tāpa-tray'āgni-samtapta-samāhlādana-chandrikā,
Taruṇī,Tāpas'ārādhyā,Tanu-madhyā,Tamō'pahā. (79)

Chitih,Tat-pada-lakṣhy'ārthā,Chid-eka-rasa-rūpiṇī ,
Swātm'ānanda-lavī-bhūta-brahm'ādy'ānanda-santatiḥ. (80)

Parā,Pratyak-chitī-rūpā,Paśhyantī,Paradevatā,
Madhyamā,Vaikharī-rūpā,Bhakta-mānasa-hamsikā. (81)

Kāmeśhvara-prāṇa-nāḍī,Kṛita-gñyā Kāma-pūjitā,
Śhṛiṅgāra-rasa-sampūrṇā,Jayā,Jālan-dhara-sthitā. (82)

Oḍyāṇa-pīṭha-nilayā,Bindu-maṇḍala-vāsinī,
Rahoyāga-kram'ārādhyā,Rahas-tarpaṇa-tarpitā. (83)

Sadyah-prasādinī,Vīśhva-sākṣhiṇī,Sākṣhi-varjitā,
Ṣhaḍ-aṅga-devatā-yuktā,ṣhāḍ-guṇya-pari-pūritā. (84)

Nitya-klinnā,Nir-upamā,Nirvāṇa-sukha-dāyinī,
Nityā-ṣhoḍaśhikā-rūpā,Śhrī-kaṇṭh'ārdha-śharīriṇī. (85)

Prabhāvatī,Prabhā-rūpā,Prasiddhā,Parameśhvarī,
Mūla-prakṛitiḥ,Avyaktā,Vyakt'āvyakta-swarūpiṇī. (86)

Vyāpinī,Vividh'ākārā,Vidy'āvidyā-swarūpiṇī,
Mahākāmeśha-nayana-kumud'āhlāda-kaumudī. (87)

Bhakta-hārda-tamo-bheda-bhānu-mad-bhānu-saṇtatiḥ,
Śhiva-dūtī,Śhiv'ārādhyā,Śhiva-mūrtiḥ,Śhivam-karī. (88)

Śhiva-priyā,Śhiva-parā,Śhiṣhteṣhtā,Śhiṣhta-pūjitā,
Aprameyā,Swa-prakāśhā,Mano-vāchām-agocharā. (89)

Chit-śhaktiśh,Chetana-rūpā,Jaḍa-śhaktir,Jaḍ'ātmikā,
Gāyatrī,Vyāhṛitiḥ,Sandhyā,Dvija-vṛinda-niṣhevitā. (90)

Tattw'āsanā,Tat,Twam,Ayī,Pañcha-kosh'āntara-sthitā,
Niḥ-sīma-mahimā,Nitya-yauvanā,Mada-śhālinī. (91)

Mada-ghūrṇita-rakt'ākṣhī,Mada-pāṭala-gaṇḍa-bhūḥ ,
Chandana-drava-digdh'āṅgī,Chāmpeya-kusuma-priyā. (92)

Kuśhalā,Komal'ākārā,Kurukullā,Kuleśhvarī,
Kula-kuṇḍālayā,Kaula-mārga-tatpara-sevitā. (93)

Kumāra-gaṇa-nāth'āmbā,Tuṣhṭiḥ,Puṣhṭir,Matir,Dhṛitiḥ,
Śhāntiḥ,Swasti-matī,kāntir,Nandinī,Vighna-nāśhinī. (94)

Tejovatī,Tri-nayanā,Lolākṣhī,Kāma-rūpiṇī,
Mālinī,Hamsinī,Mātā,Malay'āchala-vāsinī. (95)

Su-mukhī,Nalinī,Su-bhrūḥ,Śhobhanā,Sura-nāyikā,
Kāla-kaṇṭhī,Kānti-matī,Kṣhobhiṇī,Sūkṣhma-rūpiṇī. (96)

Vajreśhvarī,Vāma-devī,Vayō'vasthā-vivarjita,
Siddheśhvarī,Siddha-vidyā,Siddha-mātā,Yaśhaswinī. (97)

Viśhuddhi-chakra-nilaya,"Rakta-varṇā,Tri-lochanā,
Khaṭvāṅg'ādi-pra-haraṇā,Vadan'aika-samanvitā. (98)

Pāyas'ānna-priyā,Tvak-sthā,Paśhu-loka-bhayañ-karī,
Amṛit'ādi-mahāśhakti-samvṛitā,Ḍākin'īśhwarī. (99)

Anāhat'ābja-nilayā,Śhyām'ābhā,Vadana-dvayā,
Danṣhṭr'ojjvalā,'Akṣha-mālādi-dharā,Rudhira-samsthitā. (100)

Kāla-rātry'Ādi-shakty'Augha-vṛitā,Snigdh'audana-priyā,
Mahā-vīrendra-varadā,Rākiṇy'ambā-swarūpiṇī. (101)

Maṇipūr'ābja-nilayā,Vadana-traya-samyutā,
Vajr'ādik'āyudh-opetā,Ḍāmary'ādi-bhir-āvṛitā. (102)

Rakta-varṇā,Mamsa-niṣhṭhā,Guḍ'ānna-prīta-mānasā,
Samasta-bhakta-sukhadā,Lākiny'ambā-swarūpiṇī. (103)

Swādhiṣhṭhān'āmbuja-gatā,Chatur-vaktra-manoharā,
Śhūlādy'āyudha-sampannā,Pīta-varna,Āti-garvitā. (104)

Medo-niṣhṭhā,Madhu-prītā,Bandhiny'ādi-samanvitā,
Dadhyann'āsakta-hṛidayā,Kākinī-rūpa-dhāriṇī. (105)

Mūlādhār'āmbuj'ārūḍhā,Pañcha-vaktra,'Āsthi-samsthitā,
Aṅkush'ādi-praharaṇā,Varad'ādi-niṣhevitā. (106)

Mudgaudan'āsakta-chittā,Sākiny'ambā-swarūpiṇī,
Āgñyā-chakr'ābja-nilayā,Śhukla-varṇā,Ṣhad-ananā. (107)

Majjā-samsthā,Haṁsavatī-mukhya-śhakti-samanvitā,
Haridr'ānn'aika-rasikā,Hākinī-rūpa-dhāriṇī. (108)

Sahasra-dala-padma-sthā,Sarva-varṇ'opa-śhobhitā,
Sarv'āyudha-dharā,Śhukla-sam-sthitā,Sarvato-mukhī. (109)

Sarv'audana-prīta-chittā,Yakiny'amba-swarūpiṇī,
Swāhā,Swadhā,Matir-Medhā,Śhrutiḥ,Smṛitir,Anuttamā. (110)

Puṇya-kīrtiḥ,Puṇya-labhyā,Puṇya-śhravaṇa-kīrtanā,
Pulomaj'ārchitā,Bandha-mochanī,Bandhur'ālakā. (111)

Vimarśha-rūpiṇī,Vidyā,Viyad-ādi-jagat-prasūḥ,
Sarva-vyādhi-praśhamanī,Sarva-mṛityu-nivāriṇī. (112)

Agra-gaṇya,'Āchintya-rūpā,Kali-kalmaṣha-nāśhinī,
Kātyāyanī,Kāla-hantrī,Kamal'ākṣha-niṣhevitā. (113)

Tāmbūla-pūrita-mukhī,Dāḍimī-kusuma-prabhā,
Mṛig'ākṣhī,Mohinī,Mukhyā,Mṛiḍānī,Mitra-rūpiṇī. (114)

Nitya-tṛiptā,Bhakta-nidhir,Niyantrī,Nikhil'eśhvarī,
Maitry'ādi-vāsanā-labhyā,Mahā-pralaya-sākṣhiṇī. (115)

Parā-śhaktiḥ,Parā-niṣhṭhā,Pra-gñyāna-ghana-rūpiṇī,
Mādhvī-pānālasā,Mattā,Matṛika-varṇa-rūpiṇī. (116)

Mahā-kailāsa-nilayā,Mṛiṇāla-mridu-dorlatā,
Mahanīyā,Dayā-mūrtir,Mahā-sām-rājya-śhālinī. (117)

Ātma-vidyā,Mahā-vidyā,Śhrī-vidyā,Kāma-sevitā ,
Śhrī-ṣhoḍaśh'ākṣharī-vidyā,Trikūṭā,Kāma-koṭikā. (118)

Kaṭākṣha-kiṁkarī-bhūta-kamalā-koṭi-sevitā,
Śhiraḥsthitā,Chandranibhā,Bhālasth'endra-dhanuṣh-prabhā.(119)

Hṛidaya-sthā,Ravi-prakhyā,Trikoṇ'āntara-dīpikā,
Dākṣhāyaṇī,Daitya-hantrī,Dakṣha-yagñya-vināśhinī. (120)

Darāndolita-dīrgh'ākṣhī,Dara-hās'oj-jvalan-mukhī,
Guru-mūrtir,Guṇa-nidhir,Gomātā,Guha-janma-bhūḥ. (121)

Deveśhī,Daṇḍa-nītisthā,Dahar'ākāśha-rūpiṇī,
Pratipan-mukhya-rākānta-tithi-maṇḍala-pūjita. (122)

Kal'ātmikā,Kalā-nāthā,Kāvy'ālāpa-vinodinī,
Sa-chāmara-ramā-vāṇī-savya-dakṣhiṇa-sevitā. (123)

Ādi-śhaktiḥ,Amey'ātmā,Paramā Pāvan'ākṛitiḥ,
Aneka-koṭi-brahmāṇḍa-jananī,Divya-vigrahā. (124)

Klīṁ-kārī,Kevalā,Guhyā,Kaivalya-pada-dāyinī,
Tripurā,Tri-jagad-vandyā,Tri-mūrtir,Tri-daśh'eśhvarī. (125)

Try'akṣharī,Divya-gandh'āḍhyā,Sindūra-tilak'ānchitā,
Umā,Śhailendra-tanayā,Gaurī,Gandharva-sevitā. (126)

Viśhva-garbhā,Svarṇa-garbhā,Varadā,Vāg-adhīśhvarī,
Dhyāna-gamyā,Aparichchhedyā,Gñyānadā,Gñyāna-vigrahā. (127)

Sarva-vedānta-saṁ-vedyā,Saty'ānanda-sva-rūpiṇī,
Lopāmudr'ārchitā,Līlā-klṛipta-brahmāṇḍa-maṇḍalā. (128)

Adṛiśhyā,Dṛiśhya-rahitā,Vigñyātrī,Vedya-varjitā,
Yoginī,Yoga-dā,Yogyā,Yog'ānandā,Yugan-dharā. (129)

Ichchhā-śhaktī-gñyānā-śhaktī-krīya-śhaktī-sva-rūpiṇī,
Sarv'ādhārā,Su-pratiṣhṭhā,Sad-asad-rūpa-dhārinī. (130)

Aṣhṭa-mūrtir,Ajā,Jetrī,Loka-yātrā-vidhāyinī,
Ekākinī,Bhūma-rūpā,Nir-dvaitā,Dvaita-varjitā. (131)

Anna-dā,Vasu-dā,Vṛiddhā,Brahm'ātmaikya-sva-rūpiṇī,
Bṛihatī,Brāhmaṇī,Brahmī,Brahm'ānandā,Bali-priyā. (132)

Bhāṣhā-rūpā,Bṛihat-senā,Bhāv'ābhāva-vivarjitā,
Sukh'ārādhyā,Shubha-karī,Śhobhanā-sulabh'āgatiḥ. (133)

Rāja-rājeśhvarī,Rājya-dāyinī,Rājya-vallabhā,
Rājat-kṛipā,Rāja-pīṭha-niveśhita-nij'āśhritā. (134)

Rājya-lakṣhmīḥ,Kośha-nāthā,Chatur-aṅga-baleśhvarī,
Sām-rājya-dāyinī,Satya-sandhā,Sāgara-mekhalā. (135)

Dīkṣhitā,Daitya-śhamanī,Sarva-loka-vaśhaṁ-karī,
Sarvārtha-dātrī,Sāvitrī,Sach-chid-ānanda-rūpiṇī. (136)

Deśha-kāl'āparich-chhinnā,Sarva-gā,Sarva-mohinī,
Saraswatī,Śhāstra-mayī,Guhāmbā,Guhya-rūpiṇī. (137)

Sarv'opādhi-vinir-muktā,Sadāśhiva-pati-vratā,
Saṁ-pra-dāyeśhvarī,Sādhu,Ī,Guru-maṇḍala-rūpiṇī. (138)

Kulot-tīrṇā,Bhag'ārādhyā,Māyā,Madhu-matī,Mahī,
Gaṇāmbā,Guhyak'ārādhyā,Komal'aṅgī,Guru-priyā. (139)

Swa-tantrā,Sarva-tantreśhī,Dakṣhīṇā-mūrti-rūpiṇī,
Sanak'ādi-sam-ārādhyā,Śhiva-gñyāna-pradāyinī. (140)

Chit-kalā,ʿAnanda-kalikā,Prema-rūpā,Priyaṁ-karī,
Nāma-pārāyaṇa-prītā,Nandi-vidyā,Naṭeśhvarī. (141)

Mithyā-jagad-adhi-ṣhṭhānā,Mukti-dā,Mukti-rūpiṇī,
Lāsya-priyā,Laya-karī,Lajjā,Rambhʿādi-vanditā. (142)

Bhava-dāva-sudha-vṛiṣhtiḥ,Pāpʿārāṇya-davānalā ,
Daur-bhāgya-tūla-vātūlā,Jarādhvʿāntara-viprabhā. (143)

Bhāgyābdhi-chandrikā,Bhakta-chitta-keki-ghanʿāghanā,
Roga-parvata-dambholir,Mṛityu-dāru-kuṭhārikā. (144)

Maheśhvarī,Mahā-kālī,Mahā-grasā,Mahā-śhanā,
Aparṇā,Chaṇḍikā,Chaṇḍa-muṇḍʿāsura-niṣhūdinī. (145)

Kṣharʿākṣharʿātmikā,Sarva-lokeśhī,Vishva-dhāriṇī,
Tri-varga-dātrī,Su-bhagā,Tryʿambakā,Tri-guṇʿātmikā. (146)

Swargʿāpa-varga-dā,Śhuddhā,Japā-puṣhpa-nibhʿākṛitiḥ,
Ojovatī,Dyuti-dharā,Yagñya-rūpā,Priya-vratā. (147)

Dur-ārādhyā,Dur-ādharṣhā,Pāṭali-kusuma-priyā,
Mahatī,Meru-nilayā,Mandāra-kusuma-priyā. (148)

Vīrʿārādhyā,Virāḍ-rūpā,Vi-rajā,Vishwato-mukhī,
Pratyag-rūpā,Parʿākāśhā,Prāṇa-dā,Prāṇa-rūpiṇī. (149)

Mārtaṇḍa-bhairavʿārādhyā,Mantriṇī-nyasta-rājya-dhūḥ,
Tri-pureśhī,jayat-senā,Nis-trai-guṇyā,Parʿāparā. (150)

Satya-gñyān'ānanda-rūpā,Sāmarasya-parāyaṇā,
Kapardinī,kalā-mālā,Kāma-dhuk,Kāma-rūpiṇī.(151)

Kalā-nidhiḥ,Kāvya-kalā,Rasa-gñyā,Rasa-śhevadhiḥ,
Puṣhṭā,Purātanā,Pūjyā,Puṣhkarā,Puṣhkar'ekṣhaṇā. (152)

Param-jyotiḥ,Param-dhāmā,Param-āṇuḥ,Parāt-parā,
Pāśha-hastā,Pāśha-hantrī,Para-mantra-vibhedinī. (153)

Mūrtā,Āmūrtā,Anitya-tṛiptā,Muni-mānasa-hamsikā,
Satya-vratā,Satya-rūpā,Sarv'āntar-yāminī,Satī. (154)

Brahmāṇī,Brahma,Jananī,Bahu-rūpā,Budh'ārchitā,
Prasavitrī,Prachaṇḍ'āgñyā,Pratiṣhṭhā,Prakaṭ'ākṛitiḥ. (155)

Prāṇeśhvarī,Prāṇa-dātrī,Pañchāśhat-pīṭha-rūpiṇī,
Viśhṛiṅ-khalā,Vivikta-sthā,Vīra-mātā,Viyat-prasūḥ. (156)

Mukundā,Mukti-nilayā,Mūla-vigraha-rūpiṇī,
Bhāva-gñyā,Bhava-roga-ghnī,Bhava-chakra-pravartinī. (157)

Chhandaḥ-sārā,Śhāstra-sārā,Mantra-sārā,Talodarī,
Udāra-kīrtir,Uddāma-vaibhavā,Varṇa-rūpiṇī. (158)

Janma-mṛityu-jarā-tapta-jana-viśhrānti-dāyinī,
Sarv'opaniṣhad-ud-ghuṣhṭā,Śhānty'atīta-kal'ātmikā. (159)

Gambhīrā,Gagan'ānta-sthā,Garvitā,Gāna-lolupā,
Kalpanā-rahitā,Kāṣhṭhā,'AKāntā,Kānt'ardha-vigrahā. (160)

Kārya-kāraṇa-nir-muktā,Kāma-keli-tarañ-gitā,
Kanat-kanaka-tāṭankā,Līlā-vigraha-dhāriṇī. (161)

Aja,kṣhaya-vinir-muktā,Mugdhā,Kṣhipra-prasādinī,
Antar-mukha-sam-ārādhyā,Bahir-mukha-su-dur-labhā. (162)

Trayī,Trivarga-nilayā,Tri-sthā,Tripura-mālinī,
Nir-āmayā,Nir-ālaṁbā,Sw'ātmā-rāmā,Sudhā-sṛutiḥ. (163)

Saṁsāra-panka-nir-magna-sam-uddharaṇa-paṇḍitā,
Yagñya-priyā,Yagñya-kartrī,Yajamāna-swarūpiṇī. (164)

Dharm'ādhārā,Dhan'ādhyakṣhā,Dhana-dhānya-vivardhinī,
Vipra-priyā,Vipra-rūpā,Viśhwa-bhramaṇa-kāriṇī. (165)

Viśhwa-grāsā,Vidrum-ābhā,Vaiṣhṇavī,Viṣhṇu-rūpiṇī,
Ayoniḥ,Yoni-nilayā,Kūṭa-sthā,Kula-rūpiṇī. (166)

Vīra-goṣhṭhī-priya,Vīrā,Naiṣh-karmyā,Nāda-rūpiṇī ,
Vigñyāna-kalanā,Kalyā,Vidagdhā,Baindav-āsanā. (167)

Tattw'ādhikā,Tattwa-mayī,Tattwam-artha-rūpinī,
Sāma-gāna-priyā,Saumyā,Sadāśhiva-kuṭumbinī. (168)

Savy'āpa-savya-mārga-sthā,Sarvāpad-vini-vāriṇī,
Swasthā,Swabhāva-madhurā,Dhirā,Dhira-sam-architā. (169)

Chaitany-ārghya-sam-ārādhyā,Chaitanya-kusuma-priyā,
Sadoditā,Sadātuṣhṭā,Taruṇ-āditya-pāṭalā. (170)

Dakṣhiṇ'ādakṣhiṇ'ārādhyā,Dara-smera-mukh'āmbujā,
Kaulinī-kevalā,'Anardhya-kaivalya-pada-dāyinī. (171)

Stotra-priyā,Stuti-matī,Śhruti-saṁ-stuta-vaibhavā,
Manasvinī,Māna-vatī,Maheśhī,Maṅgal'ākṛitiḥ. (172)

Viśhwa-mātā,Jagad-dhātrī,Viśhāl'ākṣhī,Vi-rāgiṇī,
Pra-galbhā,Param'odārā,Par'āmodā,Mano-mayī. (173)

Vyoma-keśhī,Vimāna-sthā,Vajriṇī,Vāmak'eśhvarī,
Pañcha-yagñya-priyā,Pañcha-preta-mañch'ādhi-śhāyinī. (174)

Paṇchamī,Pañcha-bhūteśhī,Pañcha-saṁkhy'opa-chārinī,
Śhāśhwatī,Śhāśhwat'aiśhwaryā,Śharmadā,Śhambhu-mohinī. (175)

Dharā,Dhara-sutā,Dhanyā,Dharmiṇī,Dharma-vardhinī,
Lok'ātītā,Guṇ'ātītā,Sarv'ātītā,Śham'ātmikā. (176)

Bandhūka-kusuma-prakhyā,Bālā,Līla-vinodinī,
Su-maṅgalī,Sukha-karī,Suveṣh-āḍhyā,Su-vāsinī. (177)

Su-vāsiny-archana-prītā,Āshobhanā,Śhuddha-mānasā,
Bindu-tarpaṇa-santuṣhṭā,Pūrva-jā,Tri-pur'āmbikā. (178)

Daśha-mudra-sam-ārādhyā,Tripurā-śhrī-vaśham-karī,
Gñyāna-mudrā,Gñyāna-gamyā,Gñyāna-gñyeya-svarūpiṇī. (179)

Yoni-mudrā,Tri-khaṇḍeśhī,Tri-guṇa,Ambā,Trikoṇa-gā,
Anaghā,Adbhuta-chāritrā,Vāñchhit'ārtha-pradāyinī. (180)

Abhyās'ātiśhaya-gñyātā,Ṣhaḍ-adhv'ātīta-rūpiṇī,
Avyāja-karuṇā-mūrtir,Agñyāna-dhvānta-dīpikā. (181)

Ābāla-gopa-viditā,Sarv'ān-ullaṅghya-śhāsanā,
Śhrī-chakra-rāja-nilayā,Śhrīmat-tripura-sundarī. (182)

Śhrī-śhivā-Śhiva-śhakty'aikya-rūpiṇī-Lalit'āmbikā. (183)

All hail, Divine Mother! You embody the sacred union of Shiva and Shakti, the very essence of Oneness. From you, O Lalita, flows the entire universe, a magnificent play of your divine will.

Here ends the Thousand Names of Shri Lalita as a poem.

Chapter 8: Wisdom from Lalita Sahasranama: Transformative Potential enshrined within this sacred hymn

The Central Dot: Divine Union and Spiritual Awareness

The central dot (Bindu) in the Sri Yantra represents the perfect union of Shiva and Shakti, the divine masculine and feminine energies. Within the human body, this dot corresponds to the crown of the head, the Crown Chakra, a sacred center of spiritual awareness.

The Sumeru: A Dual Representation

The term "sumeru" has a dual meaning: it represents both the devotee's body or backbone, as well as the three-dimensional form of the Sri Yantra known as "meru prastara."

The Throne of Five Gods: Divine - Foundation and Human Structure

Lalita Devi is depicted seated on a throne supported by four deities: Brahma, Vishnu, Rudra, and Ishvara. These gods symbolize the four aspects of creation, preservation, destruction, and concealment. The central plank of the throne is Sadashiva, representing the foundation of pure consciousness.

Similarly, the human body is a vessel created from the five elements: earth, water, fire, air, and space. These elements reside within the various chakras (Energy centers) along the spine, from the mooladhara (Root) to the visuddhi (Throat), governing their respective functions within the body. This structure formed by the chakras is known as the 'throne of five gods,' highlighting the deep connection between the human body and the cosmic structure.

"In the silent dot, the soul awakens to its divine embrace."

THE LAW OF ATTRACTION: MANIFESTING DESIRES

**Ichchhā-śhaktī-gñyānā-śhaktī-krīya-śhaktī-sva-rūpiṇī,
Sarvʿādhārā,Su-pratiṣhṭhā,Sad-asad-rūpa-dhāriṇī. (130)**

This verse, from the revered Lalita Sahasranama, offers a profound description of the Divine Mother, Lalita Devi. Let's break down the Sanskrit terms and understand their significance:

Ichchhā-śhaktī: This refers to the power of desire or will. It is the creative energy that brings forth the universe.

Gñyānā-śhaktī: This signifies the power of knowledge or wisdom. It represents the divine consciousness that permeates all existence.

Krīya-śhaktī: This denotes the power of action or transformation. It is the dynamic energy that brings about change.

Sva-rūpiṇī: This means "she whose form is her own essence." It suggests that the Divine Mother is the embodiment of all these powers.

Sarvʿādhārā: This translates to "the support of all," implying that the Divine Mother is the foundation upon which everything rests.

Su-pratiṣhṭhā: This means "well-established" or "firmly grounded." It indicates the Divine Mother's eternal and unchanging nature.

Sad-asad-rūpa-dhāriṇī: This translates to "she who holds both the forms of the real and the unreal." It suggests that the Divine Mother encompasses both the manifest and unmanifest aspects of existence.

> **"Desire's spark, wisdom's light, action's flow: she is the all, where realities grow."**

Interpretation

In essence, this verse describes Lalita Devi as the supreme cosmic power who is the embodiment of creation, preservation, and transformation. She is the source of all desires, knowledge and consciousness, actions, the foundation of the universe, and the ultimate reality that transcends all duality.

Connection to the Law of Attraction

When we connect this verse to the Law of Attraction, we can understand that our thoughts, desires, and actions are forms of energy that can shape our reality. As the verse states, the Divine Mother is the embodiment of the power of will (Ichchhā-śhaktī). By aligning our thoughts and desires with the Divine, we can tap into this creative energy and manifest our desires.

Key takeaways from this verse in relation to the Law of Attraction

The power of thought: Our thoughts are like seeds that can grow into reality.

The importance of intention: By setting clear intentions, we can direct our creative energy.

The role of the divine: The Divine Mother is the ultimate source of creation and can help us manifest our desires. In conclusion, this verse from the Lalita Sahasranama offers a profound understanding of the interconnectedness of the individual, the universe, and the divine.

> "From the wellspring of her will, knowledge blooms into action: Lalita Devi, the architect of dreams, where our desires find form in the fabric of existence."
>
> "She dances between shadows and substance, a weaver of realities, igniting the divine spark within us to sculpt our destinies from the ethereal clay of potential."

BHANDASURA VADH: CONQUERING INNER NEGATIVITY

Chanting these verses on the battlefield brings a profound sense of inner peace. Verses 24 to 33 describe the symbolic battle between Lalita Devi and Bhandasura, a demon representing ignorance, ego, and resulting negativity.

The Symbolic Battle

The word "Bhanda" means shameless, while "Asura" translates to demon. Bhandasura symbolizes the shameless demon, representing a lack of moral compass and ethical boundaries fueled by ignorance and ego. This battle is not a physical one but a symbolic representation of the internal struggle within each individual.

Overcoming Negativity

Bhandasura embodies the negative aspects we all encounter within ourselves. Defeating Vishanga, infatuation of the senses with external objects, represents turning our attention inward, away from distractions, towards meditation and self-awareness. Conquering Vishukra, negative energies, signifies overcoming negativity within our minds, such as uncontrolled desires, anger, and hatred. The Bhandasura sons represent the detrimental habits that arise from these internal conflicts.

Lalita Devi's Divine Army

Lalita Devi's army isn't composed of physical soldiers but represents the divine qualities nurtured within a devotee during their spiritual journey. The army preparing for battle signifies the development of these virtues within the individual, such as compassion, courage, and self-discipline. Lalita Devi herself embodies different aspects of these virtues through her forms like Sampathkari, Ashva-Rudha, Mantrini, Bala, Varahi, and Jwala-Malini, Ganesha. These forms empower the devotee and provide them with various tools to overcome negativity.

The Struggle Within

The battle between Lalita Devi and Bhandasura symbolizes the ongoing internal struggle between negativity and the cultivation of positive qualities. Lalita Devi represents the divine spark within each individual, guiding us towards self-realization and liberation.

The verses mention the difficult process of uprooting samskaras, negative impressions from past lives. The concept of subconscious programming emphasizes the importance of addressing negativity on a deeper level beyond just conscious thought.

> "The inner battlefield echoes with the clash of ego and virtue, where verses become our armor of peace."
>
> "Bhandasura, the shadow within, yields not to physical weaponery, but to the blossoming lotus of self-awareness."
>
> "Lalita Devi's army marches in the heart, each virtue a soldier against the demons of the subconscious."
>
> "To uproot 'samskaras' is to dive into the depths of the soul, where past shadows dissolve in the light of present awakening."

CHAKRA MEDITATION

Verses 38-40 delve into the concepts of spiritual healing and chakra meditation. They introduce Kundalini, a potent, formless energy believed to reside at the base of the spine. Awakening through spiritual practices like meditation and healing techniques, Kundalini can foster self-awareness and well-being.

The Seven Primary Chakras

The verses focus on the seven primary chakras, the most prominent energy centers in the human body. While other spiritual traditions recognize more chakras, these seven, mentioned in this book and the Lalita Sahasranama, are widely recognized and interconnected, influencing our physical, emotional, and spiritual health.

The Journey of Kundalini Shakti

These verses explore the journey of Kundalini Shakti, a powerful energy within us, as it awakens and ascends through the seven chakras, leading to spiritual transformation.

Awakening: The Muladhara Chakra

Beginning at the Muladhara (Root) chakra, symbolizing stability, Kundalini pierces the first knot (Brahma Granthi), representing release from ignorance. The Muladhara and Swadishthana chakras together form the Brahma Granthi.

Moving Upward: The Manipura Chakra

Rising to the Manipura (Solar plexus) chakra, Kundalini dissolves duality and ego (Vishnu Granthi). The Manipura and Anahata (Heart) chakras collectively represent the Vishnu Granthi.

Clarity and Beyond: The Ajna Chakra

Reaching the Ajna (Third eye) chakra, Kundalini pierces the third knot (Rudra Granthi), destroy illusion, granting us clear vision of reality. The Vishuddhi (Throat) and Ajna chakras together form the Rudra Granthi.

Bliss and Union: The Sahasrara Chakra

Finally, Kundalini reaches the Sahasrara (Crown) chakra, symbolizing enlightenment. It showers "nectar," representing the ultimate goal of spiritual experience: healing, complete union, and self-realization.

> "Kundalini, the serpent of potential, stirs at the spine's base, a journey from root to crown, from shadow to nectar."
>
> "The chakras, seven doorways to the soul, where ignorance knots unravel, and clarity's eye opens to truth."
>
> "From the earth's grounding to the crown's bliss, each chakra a step on the ladder of awakening, a dance of energy and spirit."
>
> "Within the body's temple, Kundalini's ascent dissolves duality, ego's grip loosens, and the heart finds its boundless expanse."
>
> "The 'nectar' of Sahasrara, a shower of enlightenment, where the self merges with the divine, and healing blossoms in the garden of union."

ABOUT THE AUTHOR

Deepika, the author of this book, holds a professional qualification in Company Secretaryship (CS) alongside degrees in Master of Commerce in Business Policy and Corporate Governance (M.Com (BP & CG)) and Law (LL.B). Driven by a deep interest in spirituality. She enjoys reading, writing, and spending time immersed in nature. She loves to spend time with children.

The author believes this book offers valuable guidance without being preachy, aiming to reach and empower millions. Her commitment to helping others is further evidenced by her studies and practice of alternative healing modalities, including Chakra Meditation, Emotional Freedom Technique (EFT), and Ho'oponopono.

Should you have any questions, please free to contact her at **cs.deepikadhamija@gmail.com**

GRATITUDE NOTE

A Heartfelt Thank You to My Readers

My heart is overflowing with gratitude for each of you who joined me on this literary adventure. Your time, your interest, and your kind words have fueled my passion. Knowing you chose my words as companions is a true honor.

Writing a book is like setting sail on a vast ocean. Without a community of readers like you, the voyage would be lonely. Thank you for being my fellow explorers, helping to bring these tales to life.

I poured my heart and soul into these pages, hoping they would ignite a spark of inspiration, a touch of wonder, or simply a moment of thoughtfulness. Whether you found practical advice, a hint of humor, or a new perspective, I am truly grateful.

Please share your thoughts and reviews, and feel free to reach out to me at **cs.deepikadhamija@gmail.com.**

Once again, thank you from the bottom of my heart. Your support means the world, and I sincerely hope my words have left a positive mark on your journey.

With warmest regards,

Deepika